THE ILLUSTRATED
MORECAMBE

THE ILLUSTRATED
MORECAMBE

GARY MORECAMBE

Macdonald
Queen Anne Press

A *Queen Anne Press* BOOK

© Gary Morecambe 1987

First published in Great Britain in 1987 by
Queen Anne Press, a division of
Macdonald & Co (Publishers) Ltd
3rd Floor
Greater London House
Hampstead Road
London NW1 7QX

A BPCC plc Company

British Library Cataloguing in Publication Data

Morecambe, Gary
    The illustrated Morecambe.
    1. Morecambe, Eric   2. Comedians——Great
    Britain——Biography
    I. Title
    791'.092'4   PN2598.M66

    ISBN 0-356-15111-5

Typeset by Leaper & Gard Ltd, Bristol
Printed and bound in Great Britain by R.T. Ackford, Chichester, Sussex

MOR.

944558

To the twenty-eight million viewers who tuned in to the 1977
Morecambe and Wise Christmas Show, thereby winning it a place in the
Guinness Book of Records
. . . and in memory of Arthur Tolcher, who died in March 1987

'Life isn't Hollywood, it's Cricklewood'
Eric Morecambe

CONTENTS

I would like to thank Billy Marsh and Eddie Waters for all the help they have given me as I have put this book together, and Bill Drysdale who assisted considerably in the compilation of the introduction. Also of course my mother, Joan, for making the whole project possible and sorting out so much material. Quotations from private correspondence appear by courtesy of Sir David Attenborough, Ronnie Barker, Michael Grade, Spike Milligan, and the Estate of Arthur Askey.

The extracts that appear at the beginning of each chapter are from my father's 1967 diary entries.

INTRODUCTION

It was with some trepidation that in 1982 I announced to my father that I intended — if he didn't object — writing his biography. It had been pointed out to me that it was the kind of project one normally carries out after the subject's demise. To a point I could accept this, but as someone who enjoys writing, and having a father who made such a wonderful subject to work on, I wasn't dissuaded from my task of knuckling down and putting his story together.

The only drawbacks I envisaged — other than the inevitable critical comment it would engender from the media — were comparisons such a book would have with other, less savoury works such as *Mommie Dearest*, the forcefully told story of Joan Crawford by her daughter. I knew that in truth I had little to fear as that wasn't the type of book I was planning, nor indeed was able to write, as my father's life and behaviour were as impeccable as his image suggested.

Once underway, any doubts we'd hitherto had about the project were cast aside, and in fact it culminated with him giving me far more assistance than I'd expected or requested, something I shall always be grateful to him for.

The emphasis of the book was to show the relationship between father and son — when the father just happens to be one of the biggest, most highly sought-after comics in the land. As part of the promotional campaign we appeared together on Russell Harty's Manchester show. It was difficult for me to squeeze a word in edgeways, and when I did, my father, being so quick-thinking and irrepressible, cut in without a moment's notice.

Before the start of the show he had insisted on taking me down the Manchester streets, so many of which were his memory lanes.
'There's the Odeon', he pointed.
'Just another cinema', was my flippant response.

'No it's not', he said firmly. 'This is where I first saw Ernie working as a boy. He was in the show, and I was in the audience.'

Since my father's untimely death — an irreplaceable loss both as father and comedian — various Morecambe and Wise memorabilia have come to light from arduous sorting sessions in the family attic.

It was the discovery of fresh and mainly never-before-seen photographs that prompted me to put this book together. There have been enough biographies charting my father's career and personal life (indeed my mother and I are responsible for two of them). I've therefore reduced the narrative to concentrate on the fresh material in an attempt to present something new on Eric.

My father was a kind and generous man, with a great natural wit and childlike mischievousness about him, and I sincerely hope that more than a touch of this comes through to you in these pages.

A LOOK AT THE COMIC

A large proportion of Morecambe and Wise stems from Laurel and Hardy. My father studied the duo very closely. He once told me, 'Oliver Hardy was the first comedian to make full use of the camera. After Stan had done something very stupid, Ollie would stare blankly into the camera sharing his despair with the viewer.'

My father put his own interpretation on this use of the camera, and would portray surprise then delight when realizing the camera was pointing at him, as if such surprise was justified when discovering a camera inside a television studio, and as if partially unaware that there was even a viewing audience out there.

The similarity to Laurel and Hardy came about more in the early days of television than the days of pure theatre when they were more akin to Abbott and Costello. Eric Midwinter, a comedy enthusiast, remarks in his book, *Make 'Em Laugh*:

> The two couples [Laurel and Hardy and Morecambe and Wise] are nearest in style when Morecambe and Wise are exchanging notes in their flat. Their arguments are highly reminiscent of Laurel and Hardy chewing over problems in their stateside apartment. The bedroom scene, Ernie writing his plays with Eric alongside him, quietly disconcerting as always, is a particularly sharp illustration of this, for there were several occasions when Laurel and Hardy were to be found in bed together with problems of one kind or another.

Because of the innuendo of two men sharing a double bed, my father insisted in most cases in having his pipe to smoke in these scenes, so as to make him appear 'A little more butch,' as he worded it. 'Pipe smoking and homosexuality just don't seem to blend.'

It is interesting to clarify which was the comedian of their respective partnerships. Eric Midwinter eloquently says: 'Perhaps Eric's unending sexual misinterpretation of Ernie's innocent phraseology may be seen as the personification of the unconscious thwarting the sentry at the threshold of the conscious mind. In the final analysis, Eric is the clown and Ernie the stooge.'

A personal fear my father had, and one not exceptional in his profession, was that one day he would see a decline in the quality of his work; pushing it too far might even damage what had gone before. For my father had a dilemma: an active mind — as active as when he first stood in front of the ATV cameras in the first Morecambe and Wise show — but one let down by inconsistent health. And seeing some of the later work of Laurel and Hardy he felt sure that old men, like very young men, were not the best deliverers of humorous material. He seemed to settle on the fact that physically, between thirty and fifty was the right age — if there

could be such a thing when all of us are made so differently; and he was the first to point out that the veteran George Burns would have a word or two in disagreement to say to him about that!

My father had genuinely been preparing to wind up the partnership except, perhaps, for rare shows and appearances, to pursue his interest in writing. He said to me, in 1983, when deciding the partnership was getting strained, and it was impossible to find a new direction and too late to bother to try: 'We've been at the top of the light entertainment tree since 1963. You don't have to be a mathematician to realize that's twenty years, and when we first started we weren't sure if we'd even be able to run to a second series.'

It does become apparent though that it's easier to opt for the longevity of the act than the discontinuation of it. Morecambe and Wise became so established with the British public that other than for reasons of health and fresh material — very important reasons too — it was evident they could virtually go on winning acclaim and affection as long as they wanted to.

Other than the fact that they brought theatre and Music Hall to television, I personally feel they succeeded where others have failed by using clean material. The viewer knows what to expect before tuning in. Also, they had the ability — probably due to the fact they were never 'blue' — to reach all generations. On top of this the social style of their presentation is neutral.

The creation of the Morecambe and Wise partnership was a wonderful stroke of luck, or for the more religiously inclined, a thankful act of God. Ernie Wise is as aware of this as anyone.

> I first saw Eric giving his audition for Jack Hylton in Manchester. He was wearing a black beret, bootlace tie, cut-down dress suit held together with a large safety pin, red socks, and holding a large lollipop. I thought it ridiculous how anyone could

walk about the street dressed like that. He sang a song called 'I'm Not All There', then did his impression of Flanagan and Allen — but only did Allen. I've never been able to work that one out. No, we didn't form the double-act then, we had no idea of the future.

We met later in a show called 'Youth Takes A Bow', where we both did single acts. I said, 'Why don't we do a double-act together? Do you know a little joke?' He said, 'Yes. You!' And that's how it all started.

He's been insulting me ever since. He called me his little fat friend who wears a wig. He said you couldn't see the join, and that I have short fat hairy legs, and that I'm mean with money. Now *that's* not true. We never let money come between us. It never got past me! The biggest laugh was, of course, get the tea Ern. It never failed.

Do you know, in the forty-three years we were together as partners, we never had an agreement? No written contract, nothing about staying together, sharing the profits, who gets custody of the joke books. I think that says something about togetherness. You see, we wanted to do a double-act. We started off like Abbott and Costello, straight man and feed. Then slowly we became like Laurel and Hardy, two comic characters: the one with the glasses, and the other with the short fat hairy legs ...

I can recall my father feeling some apprehension when Little and Large were discovering that their careers could well prosper in television. The press were making a big thing about their arrival — rightly so — and my father was keen to see what this new comedy television duo was all about.

He was disappointed having heard so many glowing reports. I think he quite fancied the idea of challenge; of something fresh coming into their field. After catching up with one of their shows he phoned Ernie. 'What they do is fine,' he said, always one to give credit where it's due, 'but if it's the best competition we're up against, then I think we're OK for a few more years yet.' He wasn't criticizing, more revealing surprise that their brand of comic supremacy was so uninvaded; talent was so sparse.

Cannon and Ball had a much more profound effect on him, though he was quick to add, '... but they must advance their act. They can't just rely on the braces and slanging matches.'

In a way, Morecambe and Wise had unwittingly made themselves a special defence mechanism against potentially talented new acts that dared to attempt to steal their hallowed limelight; it was the ability to acquire the most celebrated personalities in the world as guest stars on their shows — and to use them to good effect.

They didn't hide behind the grandeur of their guests, in fact quite the contrary, as they subtly humiliated and frustrated them. These unique moments in the history of light entertainment reflect the stature of Morecambe and Wise, and the affection shown them by fellow professionals.

Even the likes of Sir Ralph Richardson have graced their shows. Mark Stuart, a producer and director at Thames TV, and the last one to work on their shows, recalls: 'The late Sir Ralph Richardson had some reservations. "I don't want to make a fool of myself or do anything silly".

"Of course," we said.

"And by the way, I would quite like to do that little dance at the end wearing an old mac and carrying a paper bag."

"Nothing silly?" we said.

"No," he said.

"Of course," we said.'

And Mark continues, 'Rehearsals with the "big name" guests were always a joy. Performers of vast experience in their own field would come to rehearsals with the wary expectant look of children arriving at a party. They need not have worried. Usually in a matter of moments Eric and Ernie had relaxed them and got them deeply involved in the exact science of throwing a custard pie or learning a dance step whilst wearing a full suit of armour.'

There was much on my father's mind concerning Morecambe and Wise in the last couple of years of his life. He was always partly influenced and certainly uplifted by good reviews and viewing figures, and all indications on the working front said they could do what they wanted, when they wanted, and always succeed. Yet, in his mid-fifties, my father felt it could be time to call it a day.

He was keen to enjoy himself a little, to travel to some of the places he hadn't before really had the time to see. His need to work until the accepted retirement age was, he felt, a very northern trait, a reflection of a background not renowned for numerous holidays or sabbaticals. He sensed guilt when not working or when contemplating early retirement — and this in spite of failing health. Fate was cruel, robbing him of the pleasures that would have followed the long, successful years of work. But he knew, better than anyone, that life never went according to plan, and that it is never a bed of roses. In his own words: 'Life isn't Hollywood, it's Cricklewood.'

A LOOK AT THE MAN

Pointing wistfully to a clear night sky, my father said to me, 'When you're dead you probably end up on a star, each person having his own.' I doubt he seriously believed this but it somehow epitomizes the desire he had to have everything well-organized for him.

The insecurity of his work, and the fact that he had been so successful and didn't relish the thought of ever losing that success, made him want to have his life well-organized in the everyday departments. However, he couldn't bear the thought of organizing it himself, for that would be stressful to him. No, it was my mother who ran most other aspects of his life — those away from his working environment.

He was never a 'one-of-the-lads' type who goes to pubs and clears his angers and frustrations with sympathetic mates and a pint of best bitter. Instead he would contain most of his feelings while in his working environment — the professional in him ensuring he rarely blew up at work without justification — and either withhold them indefinitely or unleash them at home, where he knew he was not going to do any harm to his public image.

I hasten to add that in no way was he a tyrannical figure: he was too gentle and kind in so many ways to have ever been like that, and I also do not criticize him for his choice of method in releasing his tensions. All people react differently to their problems, and in my father's position he had to react with care and thought, as much as anything else.

If perhaps occasionally irrational or impatient at home, he had endless patience at work where lesser mortals wouldn't have survived the pressures. And it is important to note that it was he who virtually carried the responsibility for the shows and I doubt whether Ernie or any of their producers would question that.

I enjoyed a wonderful relationship with my father, as I know my sister Gail did. Our brother Steven didn't come along until the later years so he didn't have the opportunity to enjoy as much time with him as we had, though they did share quite a few interests.

The humour element was always important to our family, which is why I think I got along so well with my father, and him being the prominent provider of it. Things must have been good between us because my memories of him are dominated by the love and laughter he gave us all, and the optimism and confidence he always maintained which were so contagious.

There are naturally the memories that

remain more prominent than others. For instance, the times he would try to kill a dull moment by poking his head around my bedroom door. 'Just come to see what you're up to,' he'd say. He would step into the room, hands dug deep in pockets, a cheery smile on his face and invariably take over whatever I happened to be doing.

Making model aircraft was a great love of my pre-teen period and I knew I'd had it once he'd seen me. 'You're using too much glue,' he'd tell me, matter-of-factly, and he would lean right across me to see how I would cope with the next piece. I would freeze beneath this close scrutiny that seemed to be filled with disparaging comments about my ability.

Inevitably he would have to lend a helping hand and I would be ousted from my seat to allow him the chance to show me how making model aircraft was really done. He would carry out this role reversal without giving the impression he was in any way intruding.

You could guarantee that a thud of a football as it was passed amongst a few of my friends would bring him running out of the house, a bundle of enthusiasm. 'Hi boys! Mind if I join in?' And before a reply could be made: 'OK, whose side am I on?'

He would then dominate the game, not really allowing for the fact that he was playing with children, while giving a running commentary that suggested he was a mixture of Bobby Charlton, Pele and Eusebio. 'I've a lethal left foot,' he'd tell us, and: 'Did I ever tell you about the time I played with Stanley Matthews?'

He was, in fact, a very competent player and had shown much potential as a prospective professional — and had once played in a Stanley Matthews side. He told me that it was his father who dissuaded him from following it through as a career because of a severe leg injury he'd once received — it had nearly left him requiring amputation — and he didn't want to risk his only son ever having to go through the same ordeal, however unlikely. My father's reaction? 'I'm only one-footed,' he said, 'so couldn't afford to lose a leg, and that's why I took up comedy.'

Even now I'm still asked what it was like to have a famous father, especially one who was so funny. Except for the sharing of him with the public I've always maintained that it was no different from having any other father. But recently I've learned that this is a rare thing in a show-business family. I've come to realize that our parents instilled in us, their children, a sense of normality and an unwritten code of ethics by which to live.

We have never lived a pretentious or extravagant existence; if anything it's been kept low-key, probably in an effort to retain privacy. Much of this derived from my father's humble background. He had to climb rather than be hoisted out of it, and it made him more appreciative of what he had.

As a ten-year-old visiting my grandparents in his home town of Morecambe, Lancashire, I recall my surprise when he told me that when *he* was a ten-year-old his sole ambition was to own a house one day that had a garden. My idea of a garden was a palatial area of well-manicured lawns and flower beds. He pointed to what he defined as being a garden, and I looked across a slab of rough grass, no bigger than twelve by twelve, with a jagged concrete artery winding through it. It was perhaps my first insight and understanding of what my father's childhood and background had been about. In my cosy, comparatively luxurious world, it was a particularly harsh, but useful, eye-opener.

During these visits to the North, I would often be taken to see some of the places where he used to get up to mischief with his pals when they were small. As a boy, however, his mother never allowed him to get too out of control — *her* control. As he once told me himself: 'She'd clip me round the ear and tell me not to go getting any big ideas — even when I'd turned forty.'

His father was an easier touch. He was a kind-hearted, easy-going man, and it seems father and son had a very good relationship. It would be wrong to say it didn't have its moments, because, like most things in my father's life, it was affected by his work — or rather, success.

I have the very vague impression that Eric resented the fact that his father hadn't been something a bit more special than a labourer, as he called him — unjustly, as his job title was Market Inspector. But perhaps because he had striven so hard to find his own success he found it difficult to accept that his father could be such an easily contented man, not needing the goals and rewards his son had sought and found.

Whereas fishing was a barrier between my father and me, with his father it was a bond. They both adored fishing and often, especially when my father was a youngster, would go out together.

The vision I have of those long, warm days spent in Morecambe — all happy days in one's memory manage to seem long and warm — is of my grandmother, Sadie, shelling piles of shrimps; my grandfather taking my sister and me for long walks down the country lanes to pick blackberries and buy sweets; my father filling in his pools coupons while arguing with his own father about the likelihood of Arsenal drawing at Leeds; Gail and me listening to Sadie's fabricated stories of my father's childhood with him in the background denying everything she said.

If show business was a very bemusing thing to George, by contrast Sadie had it in her blood — not inherited, but discovered and nurtured; the first generation in the Bartholomew family, the one to be recalled by name should any future generations of the family show an interest in that direction. But it wasn't for her own benefit. She was too late in her life to think about herself, and a woman going into such a career would have met many difficulties at that time, as it was

still considered an unworthy profession for females. Hence I believe she devoted herself to the task of driving my father to succeed. And she pushed and pushed all the way.

My father's morals and principles were always verging on Victorian, and this was something he was able to maintain in a business not noted for morals or principles, Victorian or otherwise. He disliked bad language, blatant sexuality, and, more than anything, rudeness and bad manners. As a father he saw that he had certain responsibilities and duties to perform, yet — assisted by the plausible excuse of being away a fair amount of the time — it wasn't in his nature to thoroughly follow through this parent role.

He formed a kind of compromise with himself. He wouldn't totally ignore his duties as a parent, but he wouldn't drag out the role. If there were things to say and advise me on he would do it in a short sharp way. For instance, his method of advising me on the birds and bees — he later said I knew more than him — was to call me to his study one morning, and promptly reveal his private parts. Not a glimmer of embarrassment or discomfort; but that was my father. 'Dangerous things these can be,' he warned me. 'Nothing to be ashamed of though; we've all got 'em. But you must be a bit careful, that's all.' Then he concluded by adding, 'But I'm sure you've learned all you need to from school.'

This incident always stuck in my mind as an example of his 'a spade is a spade' attitude, which I must say I always found an endearing quality in him. Of course, he realized his graphic explanation would be expanded upon by my mother's more traditional one, should I have been requiring it. His blatancy was perhaps his way of covering up a disinterest or inability to convey finer details on a subject.

The morning of the afternoon I was due to fly out to Jersey on my first holiday without parents, he again asked me into his study.

'Now be sure to take contraceptives with you,' he said, seriously. 'You can't be too careful, and we wouldn't want any trouble.' I was rather pleased by the maturity he'd placed on my young head, and didn't therefore wish to spoil it by telling him that I was only going for the sun and sea: it sounded so feeble after hearing what he considered the implications of solo holidays to be.

He was a man driven by adrenalin — that, and a love of show business, and I use the word liberally because surprisingly comedy was lower down on his list of entertainment loves. He appreciated good comedy and adored watching his own shows, but he was a nostalgic, a man far happier seated in front of a Fred Astaire–Ginger Rogers film than an old comedy.

The Hollywood era of the thirties and forties greatly appealed to him. They were the halcyon days of show business, where total escapism swamped the harsher realities of life; where if a figure moved and talked on a screen, you paid to watch it. And his knowledge of this era was immense. I think that Morecambe and Wise shows actually captured the charm, splendour and glamour of an era otherwise dead, and I'm sure this was another reason for their mass appeal.

My father was not made to be a commuting businessman in the City, following a tight routine and retaining a British Rail timetable in his head. There was certainly a routine to his work, but it was a varied routine. At the end of his day he could be reflecting on a simulated journey to Hollywood with Glenda Jackson as Ginger Rogers and Ernie as her Fred Astaire. So in many ways his work was also his entertainment, and home, consequently, was a place for peace and tranquility; he would have experienced the social scene enough during his working day.

It is a little ironic that shortly before his death he should have complained to me of the lack of friends he felt he had, yet with his line of work I thought it a miracle that he should have had any. Most of his friends were of show-business origin, and he didn't make many new ones in the later years. This wasn't a deliberate ploy but simply the way it was. He liked to shine for them, to control situations, and I wonder how often he fully relaxed in their company? He simply enjoyed having an audience, so long as the moment was right.

He was a contented man who loved his home, family and privacy, and experimenting with dinner parties and soirées could not have bettered his contentment; indeed, it may have dented it as in time he would most likely have considered it an infringement on that much-loved privacy.

My father was very careful to avoid anonymous crowds unless they were contained in a situation where he was in control. Take, for instance, a flight back from Miami to London on which I accompanied him and my mother in 1982. He had spent the evening at the airport almost incognito with his eyes suitably averting obvious English travellers, and sometimes his glasses would occasionally be taken off.

Once on the plane, interior lights dimmed — curiously making one feel one was inside a theatre — many of those fellow travellers he'd hitherto been avoiding no longer represented a threat to him; so what else would they be to a man at the top of the show-business tree, but an audience?

I was travelling at the rear of the aircraft — cheaper seats — and he and my mother were at the front. He ambled down for a chat, the in-flight movie not holding his interest. He later returned to his seat doing the Morecambe and Wise dance — hands flying above the head — as he went skipping down the aisle. He was deliberately seeking the one thing he'd previously been trying to avoid, and that was recognition — but on his own terms. As he went through the curtains that hung on a rail separating the cabins, he pulled them shut, and they could have been the curtains in a theatre, or the tabs used in the studio routines. He was safe from his audience who were seated the other side of that curtain — that 'Good night, and God bless' psychological barrier. So his need to entertain was insatiable, so long as the moment, the situation, suited him.

When in the company of my own friends he still felt the desire to entertain even though most parents dread to see or attempt to communicate with the kind of characters a teenage son can bring home. But not my father. He would often go out of his way to involve himself with them. This could also apply when he wasn't on his home territory.

Once he came to dinner with two friends of mine, sisters, called Louise and Fiona Webb. My mother was away looking after our villa in Portugal, so as a treat the girls cooked him a curry which happened to be a favourite dish of his. We all knew it would be a fun evening the moment he sat down with this young gathering and said: 'I'll just nip to the car and get my turban.' But it was interesting to notice that amidst the quips and hilarity that such situations evoked from him, he was willing, if not eager, to get involved in far heavier topics of conversation — conversations that didn't need a punchline — than was perhaps imaginable. This was even remarked upon by Louise at a much later date when we were reflecting on the occasion.

They were only isolated occasions, but those of us lucky enough to have witnessed them, will be able to recall their particular memory vividly, and at the time probably couldn't have failed to register a touch of surprise. Most of his life was filled with his own plans and career, so it made it all the more refreshing when he would show such sincere interest in other people's thoughts and lives.

Not able to resist the chance of a small gamble, once dinner was out of the way that evening, out came the cards. 'Let's make it a bit interesting and play for a few bob a time,'

he suggested. He wasn't a great card player or lucky gambler, but he knew he'd come out of it all right — he knew because he always cheated. And he didn't care how blatantly, though often denied accusations with a mischievous grin. If he lost too consistently and his cheating failed to rescue him he was quick to suggest we play something else, or that, 'I think it's time I was heading home now.'

Although a man of moods it seems unbelievable to recall holidays spent together where he would sustain being the comic for the best part of the fortnight. So where did the comic end and the man begin? This is a question I have often asked myself.

I now believe that over the years the division became less and less as the Morecambe and Wise shows contained more and more of their natural selves: the love for nostalgia, song and dance, musicals and so on. Eric Morecambe the holiday-maker, getting up in the morning and strolling around the villa whistling to himself, sniffing about to see if there was anything going on, could just as easily have been Eric Morecambe the performer, strolling about one of Ernie's sets for his plays, contemplating how he intended to destroy the slim line of credibility Ernie was supposed to be trying to establish.

He always considered himself the unadventurous sort when it came to foreign travel — though he had become keen to see cities of historic interest or great beauty. Perhaps travel made him think of the long, arduous days on the road. He was certainly happy with a base in Portugal (bought in the mid-sixties) and one in Florida (bought in the late seventies).

He liked civilized places where a plumber could be found rather than a revolution, which is why, in his last years, the comfort of America took precedence over Portugal. 'For a start they speak English', he once said when asked about his preference.

His enchantment with Florida followed a trip he made there with my mother in 1981.

Louis Benjamin, who runs the Stoll-Moss theatres and is a long-time family friend, was out there holidaying with his wife. It culminated with the Benjamins taking the Morecambes to a visit to the home of flamboyant pianist Liberace. This particular home was in Las Vegas, and was apparently stunning. Louis recalls:

> Liberace was playing the Las Vegas Hilton and invited us to his home for 'English tea'. We arrived for an occasion I can only describe as being indescribable. It was pure Liberace — from crystal piano to piano-shaped swimming pool, liveried servants hovering, ashtrays at the ready.
>
> Champagne was on ice, huge gin-and-tonics were served in giant crystal goblets, and in the ornate dining-room there were liqueurs on a table which was set with fine porcelain and gleaming silver.
>
> I surveyed the scene, nudged Eric and whispered, 'He appears to have guests coming. We'd better drink up and get out.' Not so. This was 'English Tea' Liberace style.
>
> The very next morning, a very plaintive Eric came to me and the following conversation ensued:
>
> *Eric* Louis, I am a star, aren't I?

Me What on earth are you talking about?

Eric Well, that fellow yesterday ...

Me But that was Liberace and that's his lifestyle.

Eric But Louis, am I *really* a star?

Me Come on, there's no question about that.

> To this day I am not sure that Eric was totally convinced. But we all know he was one of our greatest stars and in our memories always will be.

There is a little extra to the visit to Liberace's home, a comment my father made to Liberace which amused me on hearing it retold because it was so typically my father.

Liberace had apparently told his guests how cheap land had been when Las Vegas was little more than a desert, and how he wished he'd had the foresight to buy much more of it. To this my father responded: 'Yes, you should have done. You could have been a rich man.' Liberace gave him an uncertain look, not knowing if he was having his leg pulled or not; but then he didn't know my father very well.

My father was an immensely dedicated and talented man who never failed to extract anything less from me than total admiration and respect. This book is my tribute to his life.

IN THE BEGINNING

I have a nice house at Gorleston-on-Sea, near the golf course ... It's a rented house owned by a Mr Higgins (not *the* Prof. Higgins). It costs me 25gns a week. When I have my family with me — Joan, Gail and Gary — then I don't think the price is too much; but when I'm alone, which I am for seven weeks out of thirteen, then it's a lot to pay. But what you gain on the swings — you lose on the roundabouts. Or when one door closes they all close.

... We have just turned down the Pal. Panto. £4000 per week or £3000 and a cut. The office can't understand that we should turn down so much money: for the season it would work out at £90,000. But it takes guts or ignorance turning that kind of money down. Just writing about it and my hand goes shaky.

The reason we turned it down is because we have just finished a colour TV series for the States. Its the *first* one to be done over here. All British made, and, as far as one can say, it's been a success, so we must wait to see what develops from it: it could be nothing — but for heaven's sake one has to gamble some time. In the end that £90,000 could be peanuts — but its gone now —

My grandfather, George Bartholomew, had seven brothers and two sisters; a third sister died as a child. Ada is the only one I can recall with any certainty because she was such a character. The other sister was Maggie, and the brothers were Alfred, Harry, John, William, Dick, Rubin and Frank. John was the pride of the family as he became an international rugby player.

George's parents were John and Mary; John was a fisherman. All the children went to the National school, which later became Poulton Road School. George ended his schooling at the age of fourteen and started working for the county council (then called 'the corporation'), where he stayed for the rest of his working life.

Sadie (Sarah) Robinson had three sisters and two brothers: Alice, Winnie, Annie, Ernie and Matt. Sadie went to school in Lancaster and later worked as a waitress in Morecambe at the Café Roy. During the war years she worked in a munitions factory. She met George at a dance held at the Winter Gardens, in Morecambe and she made up her mind to marry him that instant (just as Eric did on first seeing his wife-to-be, Joan).

George and Sadie were married in Lancaster. On 14 May, 1926, they had a baby boy. They christened him John Eric Bartholomew, though he was later to call himself Eric Morecambe.

Young Eric may not have shone at school, but his gifts as an entertainer soon came to the fore. Sadie carefully cut out all the local newspaper articles that mentioned her son and stuck them in albums that today constitute a remarkable record of a journey from local talent-spotting competitions to the London Palladium. The following are extracts from two articles that appeared in local papers in 1939.

TALENT-SPOTTING COMPETITION

Morecambe Boy First

A show within a show was staged at the Arcadian Theatre on Saturday night when the final of the talent-spotting competition took place.

The standard of local talent was surprisingly high and the audience enjoyed it immensely. It was only after considerable difficulty that Peter Bernard, one of the artistes in the Variety show, was able to select the three winners, who were chosen by the applause the audience gave them.

First prize was won by the Morecambe boy, Eric Bartholomew, whose singing of 'I'm Not All There' really got the crowd going.

ONE OUT OF 100

Thirteen-year-old Eric Bartholomew, the well-known local juvenile stage artiste, who has made such hits in local entertainments, has gone a step further in his career, for he has been chosen as one of the four heat winners for the Lancashire and Cheshire area in the search-for-talent competition organized by the journal *Melody Maker* ...

Young Bartholomew was one of ten competitors who succeeded in reaching the area final for Lancashire and Cheshire. There were one hundred competitors in the area. The ten finalists appeared at the Kingsway Cinema, Hoylake, a week ago, when Eric was chosen with three others to travel to London. The other three were all girls from Liverpool.

The *Melody Maker* report of the area final states: 'Eric Bartholomew put over a brilliant comedian act which caused the audience to roar with laughter. In an interview he said "My ambition is to become a comedian. My hero is George Formby, another native of Lancashire. I would certainly like to follow in his footsteps."'

Although Eric and Ernie met before the war, it was not until the forties that they consolidated their partnership. By 1949 they were rising stars, as this review of their performance at the Palace Theatre in Bath shows.

And now I have insufficient space at my disposal to do full justice to the finest supporting programme seen at this theatre for many a long day.

First place I must award to Morecambe and Wise, two brilliant young comics, whose refreshingly new and invigorating material gave me the best laugh in years.

LEFT:
On the left side of the picture are Eric's Auntie Alice and Uncle Jack. On the right are his parents, Sadie and George. The photograph was taken at a photographic studio in Morecambe.

PREVIOUS PAGE — LEFT:
Eric's grandfather, John Bartholomew, who was a fisherman, pictured here with his dog.

OPPOSITE PAGE — ABOVE:
John again, walking along the front at Morecambe.

OPPOSITE PAGE — BELOW:
George Bartholomew, John's son and Eric's father, alongside his seven brothers. He is second from left in the back row.

ABOVE:
Eric's father at work on the Lancaster market.

RIGHT:
Eric as a small boy, not looking particularly happy about having his photograph taken.

A collection of photographs from Eric's childhood. As a toddler with his mother (opposite — top left); outside his house at 43 Christie Avenue, Morecambe, aged ten (opposite — top right); with his parents outside a makeshift tent, a mischievous humour already sparkling in his eyes (opposite — bottom left). As a boy he was a horror: with his cousin Sonny (opposite — bottom right, with Eric's mother) he used to go to the cinema and fire peashooters at bald-headed men. School was a non-event: he learnt the basics and left at the age of twelve to pursue a career in show business. The photograph above on the left shows Eric (sitting down on the left) looking like a real thug, with five equally threatening mates. Aged eleven he was obviously made to pose for this photograph (above) and by the time he was fourteen he looks less of a tearaway (left).

MORECAMBE AND HEYSHAM EDUCATION COMMITTEE.

LANCASTER ROAD COUNCIL SCHOOL

SCHOLAR'S REPORT.

Pupil's Name ... Bartholomew Eric

Class ... Grade III ... Term ending ... 9th April 1936

Position in Class ... 45 ... out of ... 49

Average age of class ... 9 ... years ... 6 ... months

Times absent ... 20 ... Times late ... — ... for period ending 31st Mar.

Conduct ... Good ... Games ... Good

SUBJECTS	MARKS POSSIBLE	MARKS GAINED	TEACHER'S REMARKS
Reading	20	13	
Recitation	10		
Grammar	10		
Composition	20	6a	He was absent
Spelling	10	7	most of the exams.
Penmanship	10	3	
Arithmetic	40	10	
Mental Arithmetic	20	6	
Geography	20		
History	20		
Science	20		
Drawing	20	10	
Brush-Drawing (B)	20		
Needlework ...(G)			
Total	240	55	

R Burgin ... Class Teacher

C.J.Brasser ... Head Master.

Signature of Parent S. Bartholomew
(or Guardian)

LEFT:

No wonder he never criticized me for bad school reports. He was 45th out of 49 — one wonders if he ever attended school during term-time. The bottom photograph shows the comments his mother wrote on the back of the report, asking the school to give him more homework.

I am disgusted with this report, & would be obliged if you would make him do more homework, as I would see he did it here.

S Bartholomew

OPPOSITE — MAIN PICTURE:

At the top of the photograph on the left is Eric's father's National Service certificate, giving him permission to leave his job as a coalminer after the war. Next to it are Eric's parents' ration books — still in operation long after the war, of course. Below is Eric's Child Entertainment licence, showing the first publicity shot he ever posed for.

OPPOSITE — SMALL PICTURE:

Eric aged nine with his first working partner, Molly Buntin. She was referred to in Morecambe and Wise sketches in the seventies: Eric certainly never forgot these days.

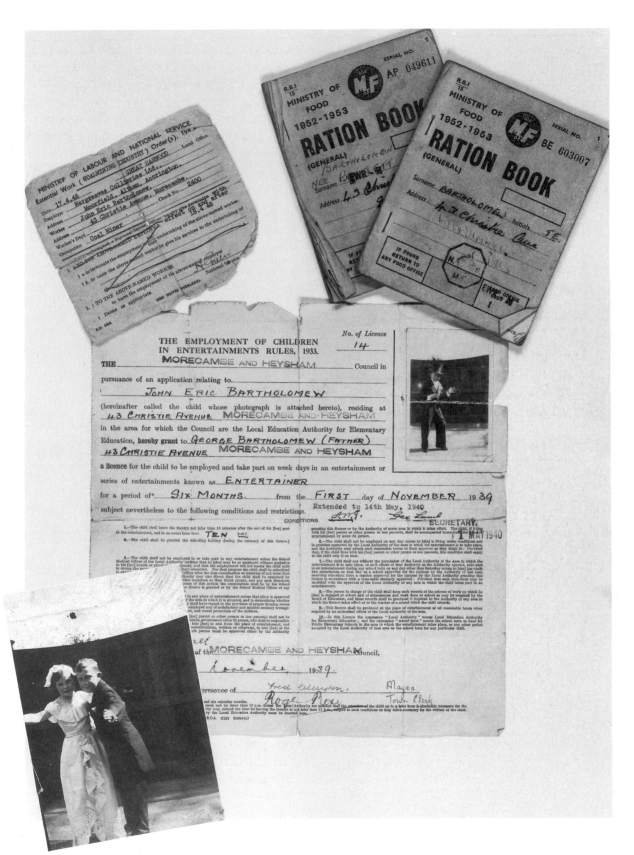

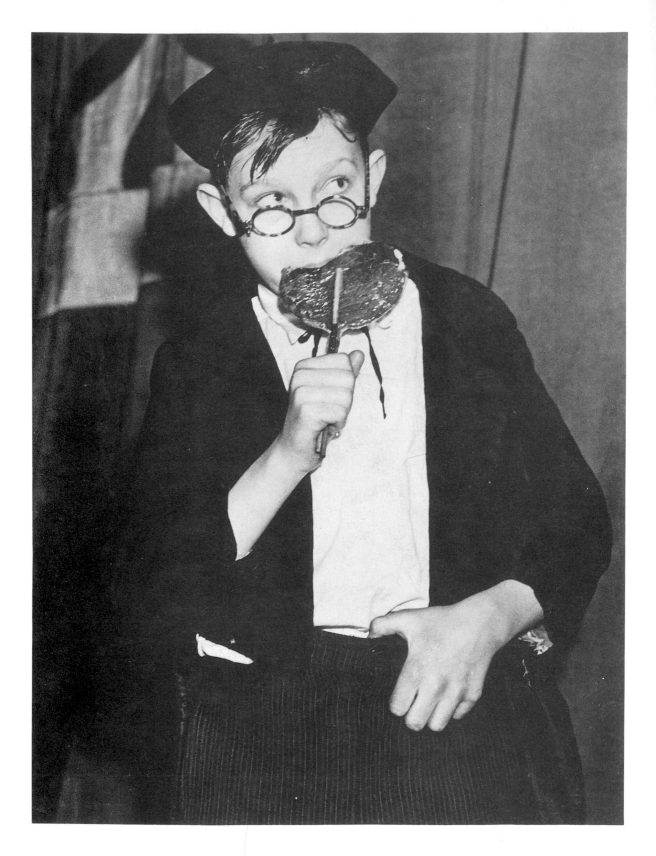

"I'M NOT SUPPOSED TO BE ALL THERE!"

ERIC BARTHOLOMEW.

YOUTH TAKES A BOW./1941.

Edwin Hall/41.

MASTER ERIC BARTHOLOMEW
VOCAL COMEDY & DANCING ACT.
P.A. 43 CHRISTIE AVENUE, MORECAMBE.

GLASGOW EMPIRE
TELEPHONES: 6434-5-6 DOUGLAS

PROGRAMME

6-30	TWICE NIGHTLY COMMENCING MONDAY, JUNE 24th, 1940	8-45

VARIETY

1. OVERTURE ... ...
2. MARIE LOUISE ... ... "Flying High"
3. PETER SINCLAIR ... ... "Scottish Comedian"
   The Popular Anglo-French Clown
4. NONI & NITA ... ... In a New Musical Absurdity
5. DICKY (LARGE LUMPS) HASSETT ... ...
   From the recent Radio Series "Phoney Island"
6. MEDLOCK & MARLOWE ... ... Dancers in Discord
7. DAVE & JOE O'GORMAN ... ... "Laughter in the Roar"
8.

> INTERMISSION
> EMPIRE ORCHESTRA
> Under the direction of Dr. HENRY FARMER, M.A.

9. MEDLOCK & MARLOWE ... ... Will Entertain Again
10. GEORGE MOON & DICK BENTLEY ... B.B.C. Newest Comedians
    JACK HYLTON presents the Most Popular Feature of the B.B.C.
11. "YOUTH TAKES A BOW" ... ...
    With Radio's Famous Compere
    BRYAN MICHIE

ARTHUR TOLCHER	HELVI RINTALA	JEAN BAMFORTH
MILLICENT PHILLIPS	ERNIE WISE	TOMMY THOMPSON
ERIC BARTHOLOMEW	DOROTHY DUVAL	EDDIE GUNTER
FRANK HINES	STAN VASSIE	MARY NAYLOR

If an air raid warning be received during the performance the audience will be informed from the stage. The warning will not necessarily mean that a raid will take place and in any case it is not likely to occur for at least five minutes. Those desiring to leave the theatre may do so, but the performance will continue and members are advised in their own interests to remain in the building

NOTICE—Photographing in Theatre Forbidden. Productions and Variety Acts, being the copyright of the Theatre Proprietors or Variety Artistes, the unauthorised photographing of scenes and acts is illegal.

FULLY LICENSED BUFFET in all parts of the Theatre where refreshments at popular prices may be obtained.

ABOVE:
Front cover and inside page of a 1940 programme from a famous (notorious, if you were a comedian) theatre. Notice the foot of the bill: although this is one of the earliest programmes in which they appear together,

Eric and Ernie are not yet a double-act, and Eric Morecambe is still Eric Bartholomew. Also note the presence of Jean Bamforth whom they worked with regularly during this period, and good old Arthur Tolcher.

PREVIOUS PAGES:
Eric's first important prop was a wooden lollipop with a bite taken out of the corner. In the photograph on the left he is performing with a real lollipop instead; this was taken when he was thirteen. The item itself (below right) is still in our family's possession. This picture also shows some early publicity material.

OPPOSITE — ABOVE:
With Arthur Tolcher many years prior to Arthur's attempts at playing his mouth-organ on Morecambe and Wise shows. 'Not now, Arthur.'

OPPOSITE — BELOW:
A very early publicity shot of the Morecambe and Wise partnership, around 1940. Two fresh-faced boys at the beginning of their careers.

OVERLEAF — LEFT:

Programmes and bills from the forties. Note the Air Raid Warning in the corner of the top one. They are referred to variously as Morecambe, Bamforth and Wise, Morcombe and Wise, and Morecambe and Wisdom — the latter because there was another comedian called Wise on the bill.

OVERLEAF — RIGHT:

A bill from 1942. 'ERNIE WISE & MORECOMBE' — incorrect spelling again and uncertain billing. Note that Jean Bamford, who often appeared as a triple act with Eric and Ernie at this time, is here referred to as Joan and limply described by the copywriter as 'another starlet'.

Productions and Variety Acts being the copyright of the Theatre Proprietors or Variety Artistes, the unauthorised photographing of scenes and acts is illegal

The Management reserve the right to make any alteration in the cast rendered necessary by illness or other unavoidable cause.

Week commencing MONDAY, 23rd NOV., 1942
6.0—Twice Brightly—8.15   Matinee Saturday at 2.30

JACK HYLTON presents

"TIME TO SMILE"

Please Note—Purchasers of Chocolates at this Theatre must tender Points for them to the attendants

1. OVERTURE
   March "Columbia's Call" Wyman

2. ROSARITA & PAULA
   Romantic Dancing Rhapsody

3. ALICE & ROSIE LLOYD
   Sisters of the Famous Marie

4. JUNE MALO
   The Charming Songstress

5. BRIAN MICHIE
   "Stars of To-Morrow"

6. INTERMISSION
   THE NEW THEATRE ORCHESTRA under the direction of W. H. COLLIER will play Potpourri "Irving Berlin's Songs" (arr. Zaloa)

7. MORECAMBE, BAMFORTH & WISE
   "Stars of To-Morrow"

8. LESLIE STRANGE
   The Famous Character Comedian

9. ADELAIDE HALL
   The Crooning Blackbird

10. JOE KING
    Joking

11. CHARLES & PARTNER
    Master of Balance

PRICES OF ADMISSION (Including Entertainment Tax)
Numbered and Reserved Seats   Boxes 28/- and 21/-
Orc. Stalls 3/6 ; Dress Circle 3/6 ; Centre Stalls 2/6 ; Upper Circle 2/6
The Management reserve the right to vary the divisions of the Stalls, Centre Stalls and Pit
Unreserved Seats   Pit 1/6 ; Gallery 1/-
Seats booked by Telephone must be taken up by 4 p.m. for first performance and 8 p.m. for second performances (Saturdays 3 p.m.), otherwise they will be sold
The Management reserve the right to refuse admission

AIR RAID WARNING
In the event of an AIR RAID WARNING being received during the performance the "ALERT" and "ALL CLEAR" signals will be given by means of four flashes of a duration of three seconds each, on an illuminated sign centrally placed just above the orchestra and below the footlight, and in view from all parts of the house.
It should be remembered that the warning does not necessarily mean that a raid will take place and that in any case it is not likely to occur for at least five minutes.
Anyone who desires to leave the theatre may do so, but the performance will continue and members are advised in their own interests to remain in the building.

THE NUFFIELD CENTRE

FRIDAY, MARCH 3rd, 1944, at 8.15 p.m.

GEORGE BLACK'S
PALLADIUM STARS

1. GEORGE STEELE'S PALLADIUM QUINTETTE

2. MORCOMBE and WISE
   from George Black's "Strike a New Note"

3. MAX MILLER   The Cheeky Chappie

4. JILL MANNERS
   from George Black's "Strike a New Note"

5. IVY BENSON AND HER TRIO   Radio Favourites

6. JIMMY JAMES introduces his Discovery
   HUTTON CONYERS

7. MARIORA and Assistant   Girl Juggler

PALACE Walthamstow
Phone: LAR 3040   Manager: VIC BROOKER
BOX OFFICE OPEN 10 a.m. to 10 p.m.
6-30   Monday, March 8th, 1948   8-30
And during the Week   TWICE NIGHTLY
GALA NIGHT, WEDNESDAY, 2ND HOUSE

Your Host of the Jazz Club
HARRY PARRY
AND HIS SEXTETTE
WITH JEAN BRADBURY

VIC WISE & NITA LANE
THE WEAK GUY AND HIS WEAKNESS

PIM AND WYN
Comedy Trampoline Act

ASTOR AND RENE
"Have a Go, Joe"

TOMMY WESTWOOD
A Song, A Smile and a Piano

MORECAMBE & WISDOM
JUST TWO GUYS

Richard Whewell (Bolton) Ltd., Folds Road, Bolton.

LEFT:
Eric and Ernie pictured with Jeannie Bamford when they were a triple act.

RIGHT:
Eric and Ernie in action, aged twenty-one.

BELOW AND OVERLEAF:
Publicity shots from the mid-forties.

MORECAMBE
and WISE

ABOVE:
Tomfoolery in Belfast.

RIGHT:
A publicity shot of Eric aged about nineteen, taken in Darlington.

THE FIFTIES

September 9

A very nice little thing took place the other evening. I came to the theatre at 5 o'clock and there waiting were two American girls . . . they had come all the way from Rochester, N.J. for five days in London — and they had seen all our shows on TV in the States and very happy to say they are great fans of ours. So they found out where Gr. Yarmouth is (a feat in itself) and came along to see the show which they very much enjoyed. All the way from New Jersey. How American can you get. Anyway a nice episode.

If the seventies were to become the successful seventies, then, I imagine, the fifties were the stressful fifties. However, my father insisted to me that, 'I wouldn't have changed a thing — other than the illnesses.'

Work was continuous — variety dates six nights a week with pantomime for three months over Christmas. Then there were the summer seasons which they did right up to 1968. They were particularly enjoyable because of the locations and the weather: as a child I enjoyed them immensely and I know my sister, Gail, did too. We would rent a house and see much more of our father and I have fond memories of long country walks together when Eric and Ernie were working in Bournemouth.

The following extracts from local papers — the first in 1950 and the second in 1951 — illustrate their hard work and growing success at the beginning of this decade.

Last year Morecambe and Wise were on tour with Maurice Fogel, appearing at the Leeds City Varieties twice, and during the winter they were in the *Red Riding Hood* pantomime at the Odeon Opera House, Leicester. In two-and-a-half years they have 'rested' for only one week, which in show business is good going.

Their big ambition now is to play at the London Palladium, top variety theatre of them all, and if they keep the audience laughing as they did on Tuesday night they should make it before long. Four curtain calls on a night when such American stars as the Nicholas Brothers and Bobby Breen are appearing, is a good recommendation.

Still only twenty-four, both boys look to have a bright future ahead of them. But it hasn't gone to their heads. Old acquaintances at home are still remembered, and old friends are welcome in their dressing room.

STRIP-TEASE AND A BRILLIANT COMEDY PAIR

If bespectacled, serious-faced Morecambe and his vivacious fair-haired partner, Wise, don't reach the top of the tree, then someone in London will have slipped up badly. These two boys put on an act which has polish and originality. Their script has a few chestnuts in it, but Morecambe can even make chestnuts sound amusing.

The pair were in *Dick Whittington* at the Sheffield Lyceum for the 1952/3 pantomime

season, with Sheila Altha, Lynnette Rae, Ken Platt and Tony Heaton. The Sheffield papers responded encouragingly:

NEVER A DULL MOMENT — SHEFFIELD PANTO SUPERB

... As 'Captain and Mate', Morecambe and Wise add lustre to their reputation as knockabout comedians of a rare variety. Their 'gale at sea' scene left most of the audience with ribs aching with laughter, and faces wet with tears ...

PANTO COMIC MEN KEEP PROMISE

A dozen autographed photographs have a place of honour today on the bedside lockers of wards in Commonside Hospital, Sheffield. They are the souvenirs of a visit to the hospital made by comedians Eric Morecambe and Ernie Wise.

Four weeks ago, just before eighteen-year-old Doreen Swift, of St Anthony Road, Crookes, became a patient in the hospital for the third time, she saw the comedians in the pantomime *Dick Whittington* at the Lyceum, Sheffield.

More Promises

After the show, she wrote and asked the comedians if they would come to the hospital, for a chat with some of their fans.

They promised and today they visited several wards and then settled down by the side of Doreen's bed to begin a lengthy session of signing autograph books.

Doreen extracted two further promises from them: the first was that they would again visit the hospital before the pantomime ends, and the second was that they would sing their 'Woody Woodpecker Song' in a forthcoming *Variety Fanfare* broadcast.

But it was immediately prior to the opening of this show that the Morecambe papers had an event of tremendous personal importance to Eric to report:

MR MORECAMBE MARRIES

Margate Ceremony

A few hours after being married by special licence at Margate, on Thursday, Mr John Eric Bartholomew — better known as 'Morecambe' in the comedy duo 'Morecambe and Wise' — had to hurry off to London for pantomime and radio rehearsals.

Eric, only son of Mr and Mrs George Bartholomew of 43 Christie Avenue, married lovely mannequin and beauty queen Miss Joan Bartlett, only daughter of Mr and Mrs W.H. Bartlett, of the Bull's Head Hotel, Margate.

Soon after the reception at Joan's home, Eric left with his bride, and best man Ernie Wiseman — the 'Wise' part of the act — for London.

Eric's mother, who is also manager for the act, told the *Visitor*, 'Eric and Joan were engaged recently and intended to be married after the panto' season, but he and Ernie are so booked up that he realized he would not have time. As last week was his only spare week for months to come they decided to get married then.

They got a special licence and were married at a Margate Anglican Church.

This week Eric is rehearsing for pantomime. He and Ernie are in *Dick Whittington* at the Sheffield Lyceum for a twelve-week season. Later, they go into George Black's show and then have a summer season at Blackpool.'

The night before Mr and Mrs Bartholomew travelled to Margate for their son's wedding, Mrs Bartholomew stuck a pair of rusty scissors through her finger. After treatment, she refused to stop at home, and went to the wedding with her hand bandaged.

Eric, who attended Euston Road School, always wanted to go on the stage, even as a young boy. He took part in local concerts before being spotted by Jack Hylton. He later teamed up with Ernie, adopted the name of his home town Morecambe, and is now making a name for himself on stage and radio. Listeners heard him in *Variety Fanfare* on Friday night.

A brunette, Joan is 'Miss Kent' and 'Miss Margate'.

Given away by her father, she wore a pale blue dress with a white feathered hat, and black accessories, and carried a bouquet of pink roses.

Matron-of-honour was the bride's sister-in-law, Mrs Pam Bartlett. She wore a black morocain dress, feathered hat and white accessories.

Groomsman was Mr Allan Bartlett, the bride's brother.

Over 150 guests attended the reception. The bride travelled to London in a red coat with black accessories. Future home: touring.

One month later the roles were reversed as Ernie married Doreen Blyth, with Eric as best man.

1953 brought the big break — the London Palladium.

AMBITION REALIZED

When comedian Eric Bartholomew, of Christie Avenue, was a youngster appearing in local concert parties, he used to dream of the day when he would be a famous comedian appearing at the London Palladium — the Mecca of Variety.

Now his ambition is realized. His up-and-coming comedy act 'Morecambe and

Wise' — he is the Morecambe part — has been booked to appear at the London Palladium next week for a fortnight.

These 'dizzy heights' meant the pair had greater publicity, including the opportunity to write their own article in *Radio Fun* magazine:

HULLO, RADIO FUN PALS!

This is Eric Morecambe calling you — and I'm doing the talking for my partner, Ernie Wise, too.

How did we gain success on the radio and reach the dizzy heights of the London Palladium? Well, it all started at school. Both Ernie and I played in school concerts, although we had no ideas at that time about going on the stage.

Later, we were asked to appear in charity shows, too, and people seemed to like our act, so we decided to take our chance and enter a talent contest as soon as one came our way.

It was at one of these talent competitions that the producer, Brian Michie, saw us, and he invited us to join his show *Youth Takes a Bow.*

We were with this show for three years, but our road to success began with broadcasting in *Variety Fanfare.* We wrote comedy scripts about famous characters in history. People wrote in to the BBC and asked to hear more — and that was our beginning.

Our favourite part — the one which we and the audience seem to get most fun from — is playing 'Captain and Mate' in the pantomime *Dick Whittington.*

Needless to say, we enjoy our job of making people laugh and would not change to any other, although a stage career is harder work than most people imagine. The only recipe for success is rehearse, rehearse, and *keep original.*

During the war I was what was known as a 'Bevin Boy' and worked in the coal mines, while Ernie Wise went into the Merchant Navy.

Our most exciting experience happened when we were on tour with a circus. We were riding in a five-ton lorry, going down a steep hill, when the brakes failed!

Halfway down the hill were traffic lights — and they were at red! All the time the lorry was gathering speed. Can you imagine how we felt?

Good fortune was on our side, however, for when we were only a few yards from the lights they changed to amber. The crossing stream of traffic came to a standstill and we shot across unharmed. That is the nearest I have been to heart-failure!

Another exciting experience was broadcasting for the first time. We were with the late Sid Field in a radio show called *Youth Must Have Its Swing* in 1943. We were almost petrified as we stared at the microphone and realized that millions of people would hear if we made a mistake. But Sid helped us through and everything went off all right.

Oh, and I must tell you about an amusing experience we had once. We arrived at a theatre and the manager, who was standing at the stage door, looked somewhat surprised.

'You're nice and early for the show', he remarked.

'Yes, about two hours', I replied.

The manager grinned.

'A week and two hours!' he corrected.

He was right! Our engagement was for the following week. Were our faces red as we went back to the railway station!

That reminds me of my favourite funny story. It is about a little boy who stood outside the undertaker's, crying his eyes out. We asked him why he was crying.

'The man in the shop just hit me!' wailed the little lad.

THE ILLUSTRATED MORECAMBE

We were just about to inquire into the boy's distress when the manager of the undertaker's shop came out.

'I'll hit him again if he comes in here *asking for empty boxes*!' he cried. 'What does he think this is — a greengrocer's shop?'

A letter in *Picturegoer* magazine was almost prophetic; it should have said 'television producer' rather than 'film producer':

TEAMING FOR COMEDY

Focus on fun men: let's look at filmdom's latest lines in laughter

Hollywood has given us Laurel and Hardy, Abbott and Costello, and Martin and Lewis. These comedy teams have brought pleasure to millions. In Britain we have a team that is delighting music hall audiences: Morecambe and Wise. Some film producer should take a chance on them.

The *Evening Standard* did not mince words:

WOULD YOU LAUGH AT THESE?

If any names are found on the heart of television's light entertainment boss, Ronald Waldman, they are likely to be those of Norman Wisdom, Arthur Askey and Richard Hearne.

These are his stalwarts in the field of television comedy. I enjoy each one. But is it not time that Mr Waldman was thinking beyond this triumvirate?

None of the three is able to do much television nowadays. And television badly needs a new comedy series.

Now I don't want to hear any moans from Mr Waldman and his henchmen, about not being able to find the artists, because I have found them. Their names are Eric Bartholomew and Ernest Wiseman.

Crazy Comedy

Mr Waldman and his customers on this side of the screen will know them better as Morecambe and Wise.

These young comedians have been seen on the TV screen three times. They will be seen again in a brief act on December 12.

I hope Mr Waldman is there with a dotted line for Messrs Morecambe and Wise to sign on. For I count these two men the white hopes of television humour. Theirs is crazy comedy which owes something to Hellzapoppin and the Marx Brothers.

It is polished and fast.

Morecambe (he took the name of his home town) and Yorkshireman Wise are both 27. They were 'discoveries' of Brian Michie in 1939.

They went on tour at a salary of £5 a week each. 'And,' says Morecambe, 'I used to send money home out of that.' The call-up came, and Morecambe went into the mines, Wise into the Merchant Navy. They teamed up again after the war. Now they top the bill at provincial variety theatres.

£150 per week

Would they leave the music hall for the fickle world of television? I can tell Mr Waldman that they would. 'There is nobody making a mark on television now', says Morecambe. 'We would like to try — especially after the fan-mail we received on our last television appearances.'

Both Morecambe and Wise were surprised at the favourable reaction of the viewers.

Perhaps Mr Waldman is worried about money; I can report that Morecambe and Wise are making £150 a week. Television could run to that, at least — if it sincerely wants new faces and new talent as much as the viewers do.

And of course the break did come, although despite the optimism of the following review Morecambe and Wise did not take off on television until the sixties.

TELEVISION CHANCE

Morecambe and Wise, the young comedians appearing in *Babes in the Wood* at the Lyceum, Sheffield, today received news of their biggest chance yet — a series of comedy shows on television.

The series will start in April and will comprise six shows, which will be presented once a fortnight until the end of June.

Not only are Morecambe and Wise among the first northern comedians to get a regular series but they are also among the youngest — Eric Morecambe is 27, Ernie Wise 28.

Their new contract comes immediately after the prediction of many TV critics that the pair will be the outstanding television discovery of 1954.

Commentating on their opportunity today, Ernie Wise said: 'It's easily our biggest break so far, but it's also rather frightening. Working for TV means starting to learn the business all over again.'

Meanwhile the current production of *Babes in the Wood* was being very favourably received.

FANTASY IN THE FOREST

... But the cooperative work of Mr Sales with Morecambe and Wise and Stan Stennett is the triumph of this pantomime. The blending of their very different styles of comedy is quite masterly.

Watch them in the school-room scene: the slapstick of Stennett, the sophistication of Sales, the mobility of Morecambe, the sly wisdom of Wise.

The *Lancashire Evening Post*, after a brief history of the partnership, interviewed Eric's mum Sadie:

The turning point in their career came in April this year when they reached the Mecca of show business — the London Palladium.

They had already made appearances on the radio and television but after their fortnight at the Palladium their appearances on both increased.

Six weeks ago they began their own radio show on Monday night. It was to have ended this week, but it has been extended for a further three weeks.

At their home, 7 Low-lane, Torrisholme, his parents spend hours readdressing the ever-increasing volume of fan mail.

Mother Manager

Said Mrs Bartholomew, who is her son's business manager, 'The lads have worked hard and achieved the success they dreamed about.

They have lived and worked together so closely that all their actions seem to come together. They even got married within three weeks of each other.'

She added with maternal concern, 'But he could do with a holiday. He's only had a fortnight off in five years.'

On 6 November 1953 the new radio series *You're Only Young Once* was previewed in the *Radio Times*.

For a long time, the North of England has been one of the most productive areas for comedy and the Variety department at Manchester has never ceased to remember that round the corner may be another Gracie Fields, Tommy Handley or Robb Wilton. Already the names of Al Read and Ken Platt represent the fruits of our labours, and we are assured that there are more on the way.

Two such people who get their big chance this week in a new comedy series are Eric Morecambe and Ernie Wise who take on the role of continuity comedians in *You're Only Young Once.* According to their terms of reference, they are to keep the show moving at high speed and in high spirits.

Morecambe and Wise are both North Countryman, who have appeared successfully in many top-line radio shows since their first microphone engagement two years ago, when Philip Robinson, then head of the Outside Broadcasts Department in the north, saw their act at a local Variety theatre. He was so impressed by their vitality and their style of humour that he went straight round to the stage door and offered them an immediate date in one of his *Workers' Playtime* programmes. Thereafter, regular appearances in *Variety Fanfare* quickly established them as potential stars, and they were carefully earmarked for a series of their own.

You're Only Young Once, as the title suggests, is composed of young ideas and youthful personalities. Apart from Morecambe and Wise, the programme will include the Hedley Ward Trio, three young men who have played and sung their way into the favour of so many listeners. A famous guest comedian will add fun to the proceedings and he will star with Morecambe and Wise and the other guests in a specially written comedy feature concerning his secret ambition.

The script is to be written by a small panel of writers comparatively new to the radio, recruited in the north of England over the past twelve months, and Alyn Ainsworth, one of radio's youngest musical directors, will be conducting the augmented Northern Variety Orchestra.

The fifties culminated in a six-month tour of Australia which acted as a bit of a life-saver to the Morecambe and Wise partnership which had been bending under pressure of routine and hard work. The coming of the sixties was to hail an altogether new era.

OVERLEAF:
A publicity shot of Eric and Ernie taken in the fifties.

RIGHT:
Eric in the dressing room of the Empire Theatre, Leeds.

Morecambe and Wise in Babes in the Wood
with Stan Stennett. Eric is on the front bench
on the right, nearest the teacher.

ABOVE:
With Stan Stennett again, this time in concert, in the early fifties.

OVERLEAF:
Are the coathanger and the shoetree supposed to be a bow and arrow?

TOP LEFT:
Blackpool, 1955. Morecambe and Wise star at the Central Pier.

BOTTOM LEFT:
In panto with Harry Secombe.

ABOVE:
Programmes from the fifties. Note that in 1955 they are already referred to as 'TV and Radio Stars'.

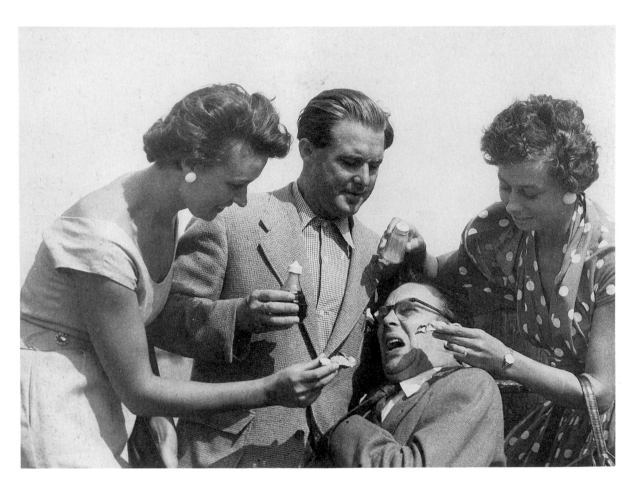

*Eric and Ernie and their wives fooling around
in Blackpool.*

On stage in 1955.

Off-duty in Belfast signing autographs in a hospital while working on the Worker's Playtime *radio series.*

THE SIXTIES

October 15

Arrived back from Portugal, and our villa over there is in a worse state than the house over here. Somehow you can't win. The weather was very nice — in the 80s. We met some very nice people . . . But I feel that most of the other residents are mostly failures over here. They only seem to be scratching a living over there. They are the ones who say 'isn't the weather wonderful. You can't get this at home. You won't get me going back.' Not unless they are deported, and I feel some of them will be. No! at the moment I'll be one of those unfashionable people who happen to love England. It's great to be back — weather and all.

This was a decade dominated by a new medium for communication — television. Having flirted and failed with television in the late fifties, Morecambe and Wise were naturally sceptical of their chances of making a success with television shows. One critic of the fifties had even written to the effect that they'd do all right so long as they kept away from television.

They had made several good appearances on Winifred Atwell shows, but in 1961, through the Grade Organization, they were given their first of many ATV series. They went out live on Thursday nights from the Wood Green Empire, starting that October. This was pre-Eddie Braben: scripts were by Dick Hills and Sid Green, additional material by Morecambe and Wise. The collaboration was a success. It was assumed Morecambe and Wise would work better in well-populated sketches, although Eric and Ernie themselves felt they were at their best on their own. But in those days they were not in a position to hold the reins, so the opinion of the production team prevailed, and in consequence the shows went out to lukewarm response.

Then good fortune struck: Equity went on strike. Morecambe and Wise, being VAF (Variety Artists Federation) members, were unaffected. So began what they'd always wanted: just the two of them buffooning on their own. And as time passed and their success grew, the scripts became stronger and stronger. The rest is entertainment history.

Constantly busy, it wasn't until his illness of November 1968 that I was able to spend some time with my father at home. There have been the summer seasons of course, but again, that was all work-related enjoyment. Here now, was a man convalescing, and increasingly keen to talk and enjoy company. As his health returned, golf and birdwatching materialized as his two favourite pastimes.

Initially he played golf with his doctor — for safety's sake, maybe. I didn't play golf at the time, but I'd accompany him if he was doing six holes alone. All I can remember is him swearing when he sliced the ball — a regular occurrence, unfortunately! It can't have been very therapeutic for someone recovering from an illness!

The birdwatching was a joy for him. He was often distant and distracted while out. He loved me to go off with him across the woods and fields, but he didn't brook conversation between us. This was a serious hobby to him; silence had to be maintained once we were away from the house.

Being young I found it hard to be still and silent for very long, so the trips were inevitably cut short. In fact, I began to notice that after the first few times I went along, he no longer bothered to take the appropriate spotters books with him; he knew I'd scare them all away with a clumsy sneeze or a request.

He did however, grow bored with birdwatching on his own doorstep. 'You get accustomed to what's around here,' he once said, 'and the thrill grows less.' But when in Portugal it was very different. He loved the exotic colours of European birds. One flew over the grapevine at the end of the garden one day, and he matched it with a bird in his spotters book; afterwards he was in a state of great excitement for hours.

Immortalized in cartoon strip in Buster *magazine in the early sixties.*

MORECAMBE GETS INTO THE SWING OF THINGS, BUT WISE THINKS HE'S TOO WET FOR WORDS!
MORECAMBE AND WISE
WE HAVE OFTEN BEEN ASKED: "WHEN DID YOU TWO FIRST MEET?" WELL...
IF YOU'VE HEARD IT WAS WHEN I WAS A STEWARD ON A LUXURY LINER... IT'S NOT TRUE!
AH! GRUB AT LAST! I'M STARVING!
HOPE I CAN FINISH IT BEFORE HE REACHES THE END OF...
MUNCH! MUNCH! MUNCH! MUNCH!
THUMP! THUMP! THUMP! THUMP!
...THE LIFEBOAT! MISSED!
CLANG!
STOWAWAY! OUT YOU COME! I'M GOING TO TAKE YOU TO THE CAPTAIN...
NEVER! I DON'T WANT TO BE CLAPPED IN IRONS... OVER THE SIDE... I MUST SWIM FOR IT!
COME BACK!
NOW A LONG SWIM TO SOME DESERT ISLAND!
"OVER THE SIDE" AND HE JUMPS INTO THE SHIP'S SWIMMING POOL! SOME NUT!
...HULLO AGAIN! SHORT SWIM, WASN'T IT?
CLUNK!
...I MUST HAVE JUMPED INTO ONE OF THE HOLDS WHICH WAS FULL OF WATER... FULL OF WATER! ABANDON SHIP! WE'VE SPRUNG A LEAK!
HERE! GRAB THESE LIFEBELTS!
CATCH! BUTTER FINGERS!
BUMP!
HEY! WOMEN AND CHILDREN FIRST!
OY! GIVE ME A LIFEBELT!
YOU IDIOT! THE BOAT WASN'T SINKING! AND... WOW! A SHARK!
AH, WELL! WE'LL JUST HAVE TO CHASE THAT BOAT! ARE YOU ANY GOOD AT LOG ROLLING?
STOP THAT BOAT! MEN OVERBOARD!
KEEP PEDALLING, SHORT, FAT, HAIRY LEGS!
4
Take a tip from Buster: "THERE WILL BE A BIG RUSH FOR NEXT WEEK'S ISSUE... ORDER YOURS NOW!"

Eric in 1967 in a train sequence from The Magnificent Two, *the last of three films he and Ernie made for the Rank Organization. All three were panned fairly mercilessly: Morecambe and Wise did not transpose at all well to the big screen. Their humour was immediate and required a live audience, and silent, extravagant locations were not conducive to their talents. The* Sunday Express *said of* The Intelligence Men, *the first film:* 'We have to watch the ruination of those two excellent comics Morecambe and Wise, in an embarrassingly unfunny spy skit.'

Ironically, with the passing of time the middle film, That Riviera Touch, *has become something of a cult. It is amazing how often people recall that film when making reference to my father; it's usually that and the Christmas shows, of course.*

*** DAILY SKETCH, Tuesday, December 3, 1963 **3**

Someone is hiding a killer

SOMEBODY is sheltering a "sick" killer . . . a killer who may strike again. It may be a husband shielding a wife, or a mother protecting her daughter.

This warning came last night from Det. Chief Supt. Bill Roberts, who is heading 400 detectives seeking the murderer of two-month-old Kathleen Riley.

Kathleen, of Bower-road, Huyton, near Liverpool, was taken from her pram outside a shop in nearby Baker's Green-road, last Thursday.

She was found drowned in the River Alt on Friday night.

Chief Supt. Roberts said: "I believe that somewhere in Huyton two or three people know the identity of the person responsible. Any such person is doing a dis-service to the community.

"In my opinion that person is very, very sick in the mind and might do it again," he said.

As he spoke, the 400 detectives—including 70 from Liverpool's murder squad and 100 drafted in yesterday from all over South-West Lancashire—were stepping up a house-to-house inquiry.

Questionnaires are being put to Huyton's 70,000 people about a slim blonde with "a long thin face."

She was seen carrying a baby in the Baker's Green-road area minutes before Kathleen was missed from her pram.

THE 007 CASE IS SETTLED

NOT a shot was fired, not a scream heard. Just a cluster of bewigged heads whispering together in the corridor for over two hours.

And then, yesterday, came the end of the James Bond "Thunderball" case. Mr. Justice Ungoed-Thomas at London's High Court asked if a "binding agreement" had been reached—the three wigs nodded.

Film producer Kevin McClory, aged 38, was suing Mr. Ian Fleming, the author and creator of James Bond Agent 007, financier Mr. John Bryce and Jonathan Cape, the publishers.

Infringement of copyright was denied and Mr. Bryce of Lennox-gardens, Chelsea, S.W., counterclaimed alleging breach of contract and return of money lent.

The "Thunderball" Case had lasted nine days and cost about £20,000.

Boatermania

FOUR men in a boater . . . but beneath the Edwardian-type turnout lurk the famously fringed Beatles. The fifth flamboyant fringe? It's a disguise enthusiastically adopted by comedian Eric Morecambe, rehearsing with the Merseyside group for their New Year TV appearance in the Morecambe and Wise show.
Picture by MONTY FRESCO.

Beauty man's body found in a spinney

MISSING beauty student, Russell Winterbottom, may have burned to death like the Buddhist priests who committed suicide in Vietnam.

His skeleton was found yesterday in a bed of nettles in a spinney half a mile away from the beauty farm at Henlow Grange, Beds.

Nearby were Mr. Winterbottom's blue track suit, a five-gallon oil drum and a two-gallon petrol can.

He had filled the can and drum with petrol on October 17, the day he vanished from the farm where he was the only man studying with 31 girl pupils.

Yesterday, police found the can empty.

Mr. Winterbottom left behind his Bentley car, all his belongings — including hand-made suits, passport, and cheque book.

His mother, wealthy Mrs. Constance Winterbottom, had flown from Santa Barbara, California to help in the search.

Mr. Winterbottom's body was found by Mr. Arthur Dilley, a 69-year-old gardener at Henlow Grange.

Life mask saves Whisky

AN oxygen mask for cattle, designed by a 31-year-old woman don, was used for the first time early yesterday.

It saved the life of Whisky of Strathallen, a Highland Cattle steer being shown at the Royal Smithfield Show, Earl's Court, London.

Whisky had pneumonia and was given pure oxygen for ten minutes. Treatment included anti-biotics.

But less than 12 hours later, Whisky won a first prize. Today, he will be paraded for judging of the breed championship.

The mask was designed by Miss Barbara Weaver, a lecturer in veterinary anaesthetics at Bristol University.

Whisky is owned by Mr. William Roberts, of Auchterarder, Perthshire.

Girl rider dies

Twenty - year - old stable girl Margaret Fern Burt-wistle, of Ingoldmills, Lincs, was killed yesterday when she was thrown from a horse at the stables where she worked in Swanbourne, Bucks.

LEFT:
The real *fifth Beatle? An unrecognizable Eric poses with the Fab Four for the* Daily Sketch *in December 1963. The Beatles appeared in a Morecambe and Wise show the following month.*

ABOVE:
Eric and Ernie are interviewed by BBC radio.

"INTELLIGENCE MEN"

DIR: BOB ASHER   CAM: JACK ASHER

SLATE   TAKE

NIGHT-INT-SOUND! 18·12·64

LEFT:
*Eric relaxing between takes on location
filming* The Magnificent Two.

ABOVE:
The clapperboard for The Intelligence Men,
*which Eric kept as a memento of their first
big-screen feature film.*

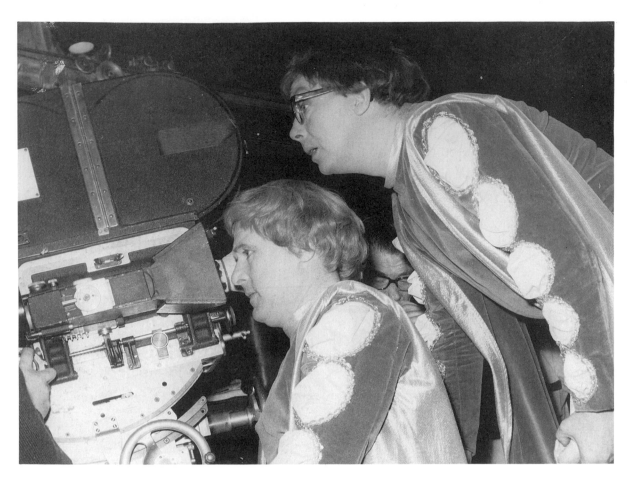

The wrong side of the camera. Eric and Ernie take a look at the set before shooting a scene for The Intelligence Men, *in which they play MI5 men in various guises.*

Relaxing during a summer season.

LEFT:
A birthday surprise for Ernie during pantomime season.

ABOVE:
Appearing on the Ed Sullivan Show *in New York in 1967.*

With Arthur Askey at Great Yarmouth Golf Club in 1967.

OVERLEAF — RIGHT:

A family portrait taken in 1982. From left to right (back row): my mother, Joan, my sister, Gail and her son Adam, Eric, and my wife, Tracey; (front row): me and my dog Bowler, my niece Amelia and my brother, Steven.

FAMILY AND FRIENDS

September 14

Gail's Birthday — Happy Birthday darling. Fourteen years old. Time goes so quickly. I feel as if I can remember every day of her life. She is a wonderful daughter and if she wasn't a little lazy she could be a very clever one. The trouble is, she takes after me.

Des O'Connor was a personal friend of Eric's despite the on-screen ribbing. This is an article the *TV Times* asked Eric to write when Des was preparing to launch a new series. For reasons never fully explained — perhaps on reading it, they decided it could damage Des' show, rather than promote it — the final product was gracefully declined.

DEFS O'CONNOR.
or
SING US ANOTHER ONE DONT.

Hello. My name is Eric Morecambe and you might not believe this, but I have been asked, no, I have been forced to write something nice about Defs O'Connor. What though can I say about Defs that hasn't been said before? He's a great singer! That's never been said before. The reason I have to do this is because he will once again be appearing on your screen in the near future. Defs is one of those performers (I must state here that he is not 'one of those', only one of those performers), that the public love. I like him, I really dont.

Now not many people know this, but Defs is a personal friend of mine. So much so that when my daughter got married he came to the wedding. He wasn't invited, but he came. Defs and I have known each other many, many years. I knew Dews when we were both the same age, and now he's younger than my eldest son, that's talent. I could tell you his real age, but unfortunately his birth certificate at Somerset House was destroyed in the fire of 1812. It was started by his singing teacher. I could also tell you how brave he is. Oh yes, in 1939 he volunteered for the army, he was only sixteen so he told them a false age: he told them he was twelve. I'll give you some idea of his age: he's got to the age where he's happy if a girl says 'no'.

Oscar Wilde's *The Picture of Dorian Gray* was written with Deds in mind.

This new TV series he is going to do is going to be a winner. Thames Television have spent thousands of pounds on make-up alone. Thames have promised that he will look younger than anyone who goes on the show with him. Hey! Maybe that's it: maybe that's why I say so many hurtful things about him. I'm not normally like that, maybe I should share my bowl, or even bare my soul ... it's jealousy. I'm jealous of his trimness — but wait a minute, I haven't got a jealous bone in my body. Jealous fat, yes. But when I do watch him I have to admit he looks good. He looks young. A sort of Cary Grant of television. And by golly he's clever. He laughs at other comics in the right places. A little too loud maybe, but in the right places. And he's very relaxed. You can tell that by the way he nearly falls over when he laughs. Women like him. Why, my jealous nature asks? Because he's pretty, that's why. Look at his nickname — 'Dimples', and it's true he has dimples. He has more dimples on his face than a Dunlop sixty-five. He has his own hair, not like some people I know. After all these years I've found out the truth ... envy and jealousy (that's a good name for a double-act). I really shouldn't let this be known. If it gets out that I'm jealous it could ruin a lucrative part of my livelihood. Yes, well then I must get back to the hitting of Dips O'Connor. I'm not going to lose money because he's good — well, good enough. Well, almost. Yes that's it Eric, you're getting back on song; say something else about him. Something like 'he's with Thames Television and all those commercials that you see and hear the voices saying, 'are you tired, are you sluggish, are you constipated?' Well he's the one they're talking about ... but I've got to be truthful, he doesn't look like that ... I look more like that than he does. He always look smart, it's me who looks as if I've dressed in front of a jet engine, not Daʋes. The reason he looks so smart is because he keeps so fit and through keeping fit has a trim figure. Mind you, he's always been on the thin side. I remember in the early days when we used to share a dressing room together he was thin, as a matter of fact he was one of the thinnest people I had ever seen. Maybe I shouldn't tell you this, but in those days he used to wear braces to keep his underpants up. And one time we were locked in the dressing room and he used his nose to pick the lock ... which is better than the other way round!

There's something else I must say. I've never heard him say anything even a little bit nasty about me. When I was ill he sent me flowers and a get-well card. When he was in hospital having something done to his leg I did all sorts of terrible things ... I phoned the surgeon telling him to take it off. I sent him a keep-ill card. I sent flowers in the shape of a wreath. But my friends tell me he says all sorts of nice things about me. The only consolation I get out of that is that they are lies. I'm not nice. Well, I've found out something ... he tells lies about me. But when I look back at some of the things I've said about him, things like 'He suffers with athlete's throat ... when he sings, you want to run'. Oh dear, oh dear. And, 'When a fight starts, he always does his best ... a hundred yards in ten seconds'. Or, 'He can fall asleep while running for a bus'. And what about, 'The last time I saw a face like that, Tarzan was feeding it bananas! He went on after the monkey act and the audience thought it was an encore!' 'What a voice, he couldn't carry a tune if it had handles' ... I feel ashamed, I really doɳ̸t́. But what should I do about it? Should I maybe, apologize? But how can I ... As I said before, there's the career to think of, and the money ...

greed and avarice (another good name for a double-act) has set in. I could forget about Daʋes and find someone else to vent my venom on, but then I might pick on someone who would fight back, and I sure as anything don't want that. It's not that I'm a coward, it's that I'm too old now to start hitting back. Now if I was the same age as Duʋs I'd be better prepared. No ... after not a lot of thought the conclusion is the same, 'better the singer you know than the singer you don't know'. So OK, here we go again ... Nothing personal Daʋes.

A certain singer/comedian (he's only funny when he's singing), will be on your screens soon. He will be fronting a chat-type show and the show and the audience will be live until the compere starts singing. The show is being presented by Thames Television because they couldn't get Michael Parkinson to sing (who, incidently, is a worse singer than Duʋs). Thames are proud to be able to present the show with this great entertainer; already they have a large picture in the corridor on the way to the bar. Now that reminds me, I've never seen my old pal the worse for drink. Never. He's never had the glazed look. The only time I've seen a twinkle in his eye was when the sun caught his bifocals. But to get back to Thames and the large picture in the main corridor ... he looks about seventeen. But why not, when that picture was taken he was seventeen. He has been placed alongside some of the immortals of show business. Marie Lloyd ... Harry Champion ... Will Fyffe ... He knew them all. He looks handsome in that picture: his own hair, his own teeth, and somebody else's suit. The pity is that the picture isn't in colour. But you can't have everything. If they didn't do colour pictures in those days they didn't do them, and that's all there is to it. So there we are. It's amazing the things you find out about yourself once you commit yourself to paper. I never remotely realized that I like Dukes so much. I must also make a point of listening to a record of his that someone sent me as a gag; it was one of his first records. It's on a cylinder. Well folks, don't forget to watch the new Tom O'Connor show. I am told by an undertaker friend that Des is breaking new ground and as always he is worth a look.

Dear Des,
I was asked if I would do an article about you, and seeing that we are such good friends, I said 'Of course' ... which takes longer to say than 'yes'. I am looking forward to seeing you on TV again. I thought your last series for Thames was almost excellent. You really have got the compering bit off to a fine art. Anyway, I wish you every success with your new venture; you have got more nerve than me, doing a live show. I'll tell you something, Des: if the public knew about this letter, bang would go another illusion! Oh yes, and my daughter Gail wants to know if she could have a picture of you signed personally to her. And that goes for my two boys, Gary and Steven. Joan ('er indoors) says thanks for the last picture and your latest record. She never stops playing it. Well once more, take care and see you soon.
luv

Eric

Dear Lads,

Re grinning Des O'Connor on your Programme. You

missed out the greatest squelcher line when he said:

"Can I sing on your Show?"

The answer was:

"Sing on our Show? You can't sing on your own Show".

Thought you ought to know.

Love, Light and Peace,

Spike

Spike Milligan

ABOVE:

Madame Tussauds honours Morecambe and Wise. Not a very good likeness: Eric's model looks more like Cliff Michelmore.

OVERLEAF:

Eric guesting on his favourite singer's show; Des appears reluctant about something. Des and Eric go back many years and were firm friends. It never failed to surprise the two of them how seriously some people took the mock antagonism they developed.

LEFT:

A letter from Spike Milligan. Eric was a great admirer of Spike's work and felt that he was one of the few comedians who deserved to be called a genius.

BBC Television Centre London W12

BROADCASTS LONDON·W1 · INTERNATIONAL TELEX 22182 · TEL. 01-743 8000

6th May 1970

Dear Eric,

After all those sleepless nights being kept awake by the sound of tinkling glasses and merry laughter and the stench of cheap cigar smoke seeping underneath my bedroom door, I returned home to get a little rest, and what do I find? — my nights are equally sleepless because I am haunted by the vision of Britain's premier comedian wandering innocently through Greater London, under the blissful impression that the birds of prey he saw snatching fish from the surface of the Lake of Geneva were ospreys. And all because of me!

I said 'ospreys' before seeing the bird because I could think of no other fish-catching bird of prey. When I saw the bird itself, my heart contracted and turned to stone, for I knew that it couldn't be. I confessed this to you by saying that I wasn't sure; but I couldn't go any further because I couldn't think of any other species that fitted the bill. The answer occurred to me at 28,000 feet somewhere over Dijon — the Black Kite. On reaching home, I sped to my reference books. And there in black and white was the statement that the Black Kite in Europe haunted lakesides and actually caught fish from the surface of the water. So now I have told you. So now misinformation has been corrected. So now can I get some sleep?

It was great being with you.

Yours sincerely,

David

(David Attenborough)

LEFT:
Eric pictured with a very good-looking young man — oh sorry, I didn't realize it was me.

ABOVE:
A letter from David Attenborough, who apparently misled Eric with some information about birds they saw in Switzerland.

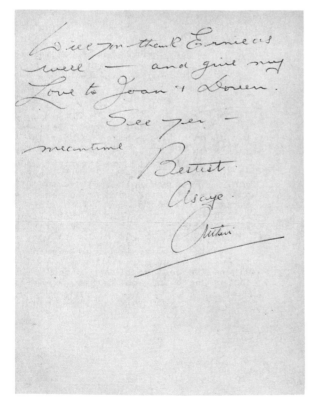

ARTHUR ASKEY
(*GENTLEMAN.*)

Home for Aged Gentlefolk.
Dagenham.
14.11.72.

Dear Eric

The Superintendent let me stay up on Saturday night to hear the Parkinson Show as you had instructed.

I picked you out right away and enjoyed your off-hand sayings very much. What you said about me was all so true - it's nice to hear someone else saying it instead of me. I thought the lady on the programme rather clashed with Ernie - her frock made me think about that joke about the "warm spoon".

Anyway, it was all worth while staying up for and I still say you are the best double-act since Webster Booth and Ann Ziegler.

Quite sincerely, mate -

I did appreciate your nice remarks - It's surprising the people who have mentioned it, so I wasn't the only one allowed to stay up late!

Will you thank Ernie as well — and give my love to Joan & Doreen.

See yer -

meantime

Bestest.

Asaye.

Arthur

LEFT AND BELOW:
Arthur Askey was highly respected throughout show business. Theatrical agent Billy Marsh told me that Arthur was in some doubt as to whether he was a comedian or an entertainer. Apparently he found out which when doing a show that included Tommy Trinder and Sir Ralph Richardson.

Sir Ralph asked Arthur, 'Are you going to announce me, or is Mr Trinder?'

'I am', replied Arthur.

'Oh good', said Sir Ralph, 'I wouldn't like to be announced by a comedian.'

This letter is an illustration of the camaraderie that existed between Arthur and Eric.

TOP RIGHT:
From left to right: Frankie Vaughan, Vera Lynn, Arthur Askey, Eric and Ernie.

BOTTOM RIGHT:
Golfing with Arthur Askey during their summer season in Great Yarmouth in 1967.

Eric adored the two Ronnies, and in particular struck up a long-lasting friendship with Ronnie Barker. They made an amusing pair, inspiring each other to be very silly.

ABOVE:
Ronnie Barker doing his utmost to give the impression that he is a Morecambe and Wise fan.

LEFT:
A letter from Ronnie to Eric. The postcard he refers to is an old one he discovered showing Harpenden, where Eric lived, which he is enclosing as a gift.

RIGHT:
Another letter from Ronnie — he was obviously delighted with the quotation.

Ronnie Barker

Flindee
5.4.83

My dear Eric — I enclose a Harpenden card (sent originally to Miss A. Bangs, I notice) and also one of the cards you kindly sent me. Could you please sign it and send it back? I would appreciate it if you could also include a recent passport-size photo and any spare money you may have —

Yours, Ronnie

From London Weekend Television

Station House Harrow Road Wembley Middlesex (next to Stonebridge Park Station) Telephone 01-902 8846

8th December 1983

Dear Eric,

Thanks for your funny letter - Joy and I found it very warming. We lit it, and both sat round the ash-tray as it burned merrily, Joy cracking nuts, and me fooling around with my jokes. Or was it the other way round. I can't remember. All I know is, I too sat in my office and looked round. So I decided to go on a diet; because if, as you say, show business is disappearing, then part of me wants to go with it. It's a fat-free diet, but if you eat baked beans and there's an R in the month, it's something entirely different.

How are you? And what is more important, who are you? Do you ever sit and think, or do you do it best lying down? Do you ever feel that you are just half of a double act called Morecambe and Wise? Or do you feel that you are part of a much larger concern, such as Morecambe Wise Dozey Beaky Mick and Tich?

Ah well, winter draws on. If not, do so at once. As to the question of dinner at your place, why not this winter? I think

London Weekend Television Limited

Arden Crawley (Chairman), Michael Peacock (Managing Director), Dr. Tom Margerison (Deputy Managing Director), The Hon. David Astor, Cyril Bennett, The Lord Campbell of Eskan, Sir Christopher Chancellor, Lord Crowther, Lord Hartwell, David E. C. Hawkins, Clive Irving, Sir Geoffrey Kitchen, Duncan McNab, The Hon. David Montagu, Guy Paine, G.H. Ross Goobey, Sir Donald Stokes, Arnold Weinstock.

2.

Shakespeare got it right when he wrote:-

IV.

When all aloud the wind doth blow,
And coughing drowns the parson's saw,
And birds sit brooding in the snow,
And Marian's nose looks red and raw,
When roasted crabs hiss in the bowl,
Then nightly sings the staring owl,
To-who;
Tu-whit, to-who, a merry note,
While greasy Joan doth keel the pot.

Arm. The words of Mercury are harsh after the songs of Apollo. You, that way:
we, this way. [Exeunt

(Apart from the last gag, which was feeble, and Burbage always muffed it. Some nights he went one way, other nights he went the other way. Eventually he went the other way completely, and had to be put in the Ann Hathaway home. I have cut the gag, as you see).

Referring to the above text, I'm not sure whether the Parson's is Nicholas Parsons, and indeed, which part of him is sore. I do know that the Marion referred to is Marion Montgomery, as her husband, Laurie Holloway, is referred to as her "nose", because of his Jewish persuasion. (Incidentally, who is it that goes round persuading people to be Jewish?) The rest of the poem obviously refers to dinner at your place, clearly portraying

3.

yourself "staring owl", and your good lady "greasy Joan" as she keels the pot. Although I am no lover of sea-food, "crabs hissing in the bowl" I don't mind, provided thats all they _are_ doing, and it's not a misprint.

Have a wonderful Christmas, and a healthy and happy New Year.

Love,

Ronnie

P.S. I have just learned that Joan has been spotted actually _advertising_ for people to come to dinner - is this true?

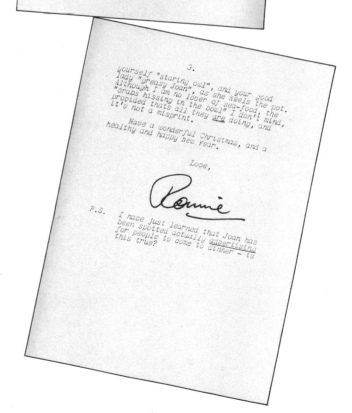

ABOVE:
At Thames with lifelong friend Tommy Cooper. The three had been on many a bill together in the forties and fifties.

RIGHT:
A congratulatory letter from Michael Grade, at that time Deputy Controller of Entertainment Programmes at London Weekend Television.

OVERLEAF:
My sister Gail was a bridesmaid at Roy Castle's wedding. Here she is with the bride and groom and Harry Secombe.

London Weekend Television

South Bank Television Centre, Kent House, Upper Ground, London SE1 9LT. (Registered Office)
Telex: 918123. Cables: Weekendtel London SE1. PBX Telephone: 01-261 3434.

Direct Line: 01-261 — 3060

Eric Morecambe & Ernie Wise,
"Bracefield",
Redborn Lane,
Harpenden,
<u>Herts.</u>   29th December '75

Dear Eric & Ernie

    What can I say?, it was absolutely, wasn't it?
I mean compared to the last one it was just, well, I mean,
everybody says the same thing.

    In every department the show was just, you know.

    In real terms, I can't put it off any longer
the Christmas show was absolutely. I just have to
admit it.

Yours

Michael (a legend in his own mind)

<u>Michael Grade</u>

P.S.

It really was a fantastic show

LEFT:
Eric and Joan at home in Harpenden.

BELOW:
Big sister mothering baby brother — Gail and me.

Eric with proud parents.

ABOVE:

A birthday surprise for Graham Hill, sadly not long before his tragic death in a light aircraft. Graham was a personal friend; Eric had gone with him to the Formula One meetings on several occasions. Ernie and Henry Cooper assist in the blowing out of the candles ceremony, while family and friends look on.

RIGHT:

Jack Warner as Dixon of Dock Green. Jack was a friend of Eric's long before he donned the blue uniform and said 'Evening all'.

OVERLEAF:
Relaxing in the garden at home.

To
Eric
to
Joan

With affectionate best wishes
Sincerely
Jack Warner
'Sgt. Dixon'

Glasses were a major part of the Eric Morecambe image, as with so many comedians (Jack Benny and Harold Lloyd, for instance). The following six pages illustrate how often he created a joke by using his glasses.

ABOVE:
With a rather serious-faced toddler.

RIGHT:
Finding out what a pair of glasses tastes like.

LEFT:
A still from Night Train to Murder, *a film made by Thames and the last thing Morecambe and Wise were to work on.*

ABOVE:
Two men and their dogs.

TOP LEFT:

Having severed Ernie's leg (Ernie concealing the pain through a tight-lipped grin), Eric checks his glasses still fit the place they grew accustomed to during the sixties ATV shows.

BOTTOM LEFT:

During his life Eric was the owner of some fifty pairs of glasses. The ones illustrated here are particularly memorable. The bottom pair were his final ones, and working up the page: a pair from the late seventies; the early sixties look (ATV days); bifocals for writing his novels; a faithful pair he wore through the peak BBC years of the seventies, and convertible tinted fishing glasses he rarely went on the river without.

The pipes illustrated are three favourites out of a collection that numbered somewhere around 100. Most of his pipes had to be restemmed at frequent intervals, as he insisted on smoking throughout all Luton Town football matches. His nerves were such that he could gnaw through a stem a match — and that was when they won!

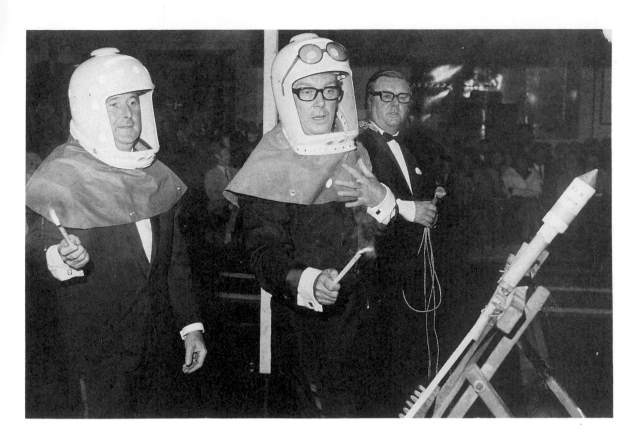

ABOVE:
*Switching on the illuminations in Morecambe
in 1969.*

THE SEVENTIES

November 27

New York. Ernie's birthday. I haven't as yet bought him anything but will — probably something small. Like a small TV set (joke). Did the show last night — OK, but really its like hitting your head against a brick wall. This can do us not much good. But this money is good — $9000 with tips (joke)

Morecambe and Wise toured the country during the seventies doing live dates. My father called them bank raids because they never stayed around for long. They drove to the venue independently, did the show, said goodbye, and left independently.

The material they used had hardly altered since the fifties and sixties, and by the late seventies he felt it had run its course and that it was getting stale. Either they could rewrite and incorporate a whole new routine of fresh material, or stop touring the one-nighters. They chose to stop touring, largely because fresh, high-quality material was so difficult to come by.

The seventies was their decade. The nation took them to their hearts, and they were known as the court jesters because of the Royal Family's apparent approval of their shows. It was apt that it was the decade they were honoured with OBEs.

Countless wonderful series were rounded off each year with a Christmas show: a show that I notice still crops up during that festive period.

It was written by a television critic that the years leading up to the seventies were a dress-rehearsal for them for that decade. The eighties were far from unsuccessful after their move to Thames in 1978, but the move itself signified change and subsequently the end of an era.

The move from the BBC to commercial TV involved more than money: it involved the opportunity to make a television movie. This they did — *Night Train to Murder* — and although I wasn't alone in thinking it reasonably good, my father couldn't be cajoled into sharing such optimism. He thought it quite awful, and as a comedian, held himself responsible. I wished it had never been done, for it is sad to reflect that it was the last thing he and Ernie worked on together. There were future shows planned for 1984, but, of course, they were never to be.

During the seventies Eric became increasingly interested in writing. In 1979 he had a novel published called *Mr Lonely*, followed by two children's books, *The Reluctant Vampire* and *The Vampires Revenge*, and at the time of his death he was in the middle of another novel, *Stella*, which I later completed and had published in October 1986. 'The Last of the Summer Whine' is an article on dieting he wrote but never published. He was planning to write several such articles to sell to magazines as a sort of sideline to novel writing.

THE LAST OF THE SUMMER WHINE

Three little words; that's all they are, just three little words: 'Lose Weight Diet'. Fourteen letters that make up the most read three little words including such classics as, 'I Love You', 'It's Your Round', 'Not Tonight, Headache', 'This is Yourlife'. Surprisingly, even 'Money, Money, Money' fails to achieve the same impact that 'Lose Weight Diet' manages to do.

Why, you may ask, and I may well tell you. There are more millions of pounds attached to those three little words than there are boobs in a Benny Hill show. Now the clever and most lucrative way to encourage you to shed excess weight is to persuade you to visit a health farm, where you can lose those many pounds in picturesque, wonderful surroundings. But, and here's the rub, they know that when you leave you will surely return because being a human being, within a few short months all those shedded pounds will have crept back on again. There is only one way to ensure the weight is lost permanently — death! But let's face facts, that way is a little drastic, even if you would save money!

Almost everything you listen to, watch or read is designed to show you how to increase your weight: cookery programmes on TV, adverts on drink, placards on the roadside telling you not to be

Guinnless. However, in between all of this emerge programmes, adverts and placards instructing you in the most efficient ways in which to lose weight. One of the most famous is the Weight Watchers. They do a marvellous job in removing your unwanted fat, their secret weapon being embarrassment. You stand up and tell your fellow sufferers that you sneaked in an extra slice of bread that week, and this makes you feel ashamed and you swear to yourself that you will never eat an extra slice again. Once you have mastered that extra slice, you leave Weight Watchers and sit back watching the weight returning in the comfort of your own kitchen. You feel too embarrassed to pay another visit to Weight Watchers and tell them again how you allowed yourself that extra slice. Instead you seek comfort from a newspaper that tells you to try the avocado diet. Eat thirty-six avocados and within an hour you will have lost eleven pounds. Or, the 200 a day banana and coconut diet: within a week you will have lost only six ounces, but you will be amazed at the way you can now climb trees.

The people who are making money from and out of you are rubbing their hands together like Uriah Heep at a money-counting contest. You have lost the weight once and now you're in for the second go. Also, you will in all probability have talked a friend (usually a first-time dieter) into doing it with you. Conversations like this can be heard in many kitchens.

'I was going to join a keep fit class, Ingrid.'
'Oh really?'
'Yes. Just to get a few pounds off.'
'Just to get a few pounds off who?'
'In weight, Ingrid. But I don't want to go alone, and I was thinking you look as if you could do with losing a few ounces; about six hundred and ninety.'
'Yes. You could be right Fern, because only last week Henry [husband] said the

same thing.' She also thought 'So did Trevor' [someone Henry knows nothing about, but that's another article].
'Let's go together then, Ingrid!'
'Alright, Fern!'

Please don't assume that I believe it is only women who want to lose weight. Men are just as keen except they hide it behind strong exercise. They want to lose weight at the same time as building muscles, a very difficult thing to do. They then start to exercise with barbells, cowbells, dumbells, and sleighbells, and before you can say 'strained ligament' they are into jogging. That's when these strange creatures go out alone late at night along the darkest road they can find, trying to frighten motorists to death by just missing their cars. They are suitably dressed for their activity. They wear shorts, vest, ankle socks and running shoes. To spend about thirty pounds in sterling to lose three pounds in weight is about average for the course.

The male starts off jogging round the block — once! It almost kills him.
'Is that you dear?' the wife shouts down on his triumphant return.
'Aaaargghhhh,' he asthmatically breathes back.
'Pardon darling?'
'Aaaaarrgghhhh', he screams.
'I should have given you that letter to post.'
'Aaaaarrgghhhh', he says crawling on his knees. He is now sitting at the bottom of the stairs watching his thighs twitching on their own.

His wife is upstairs in bed waiting. For the first time in weeks she is waiting. She thinks that the jogging will have done him the world of good and that within the next few moments she is going to see come through that bedroom door a man full of purpose, virility and lust. What she in reality sees is a man with no purpose, even less virility and more list than lust. In his bright yellow shorts and vest, a mass of quivering, sweating jelly, lemon jelly, a bright lemon jelly, he says, 'I think I'm going to be sick.' His wife peers at him through half closed eyes as he wobbles to the bathroom, her bottom lip pouting low enough to balance a half of bitter on.

Why does everybody want to be thin? Why have we got to live in a thin world? Plump is now a word you only hear at Christmas when the chicken or turkey is being described. Not everybody wants to join the Thinites, surely? I'm positive that men who visit pubs and bars regularly don't wish to take on emaciated proportions. To them a balanced diet is a gin-and-tonic in one hand and a whisky in the other. In my local I heard, 'What's yer husband gettin' fer Christmas, dear?' The reply, 'Bald and fat!'

What about Harry Secombe? Let's take a look at Harry, if we can find him. I remember Harry when you couldn't miss seeing him if he was at one end of the country and you were at the other. Now you could only just see him if you were in the same bed together. He has lost ninety pounds, which is only thirty-six pounds less than my wife weighed when we got married. Thirty-six pounds isn't much; I've caught bigger fish than that. You see, with weight you have got to consider what causes it. Always try to remember, 'we are what we eat'. So after the last meal I've just eaten I am a combination of cereal binder, sodium caseinate, sodium phosphates, sodium nitrite and the best things of all, a slight touch of monosodium glutamate, edible fat, starch, hydrolysed vegetable protein, emulsifier, flavouring, colour, silica, preservative and antioxidants. And they put a government health warning on a packet of cigarettes. I would like to meet the man who put all those things into one packet or tin of food, because that man could solve all our parking problems.

What about the hazy, lazy days of our youth when your sister said something like, 'I've just met ever such a jolly man; ever so cuddly, and he smiles and laughs all the time.' Not nowadays. The same sister in 1984 says, 'I met this great big fat guy. A disgusting slob.' What has happened between '34 and '84? I'll tell you. That ever so cuddly, jolly, always laughing and smiling man has become an object for ridicule and abuse. Take Cyril Smith. Cyril Smith is the epitome of the jolly, ever so cuddly, smiling politician. He has everything going for him, in front of him and behind him. It must be obvious to all that our Cyril is more than a little overweight. In the first place he eats too much, and in the second place he eats too much as well. But isn't it wonderful to see him laughing? So much of him has such a good time. Look at all those chins he has. He has more chins than a Chinese phonebook, but he exudes happiness.

He is the opposite of Keith Joseph. Keith is a Thinite and has that very sad look. If you were permitted the honour of being in the same Turkish bath as the two of them and watched them strip to go into the pool, well, with Cyril you would see something like Orca the whale, but with Keith it would be like watching the unveiling of a golf iron.

The fashion is still to be thin. All models are slim, bordering on thin. They have to be to get the work. Some of them are as thin as a whisper. Yet it is these thin things that dictate to you fatter things what you must wear. They tell the girl in the high street and the woman in the high heels. Those thin female models affect all our lives because they affect our wives. My wife looks at these almost invisible people, who, if it wasn't for their Adam's apple would have no shape at all, and says, 'I have nothing to wear'. Yet she has three wardrobes to keep it in.

I have to be truthful and confess to every

now and again being compelled to go on a diet. I visit my doctor for the usual check-up and he always tells me to lose six pounds. Even if I've put ten pounds on he still says lose six pounds, Or if I've dieted and lost twelve pounds he still says lose six pounds. Some doctors tell you only to lose four pounds and some only two, but mine is a six-pound man. Anyway, he's retiring soon and then I'm going to get myself a two-pound man.

As I said earlier, there is money to be made from getting people to diet. There is also a fortune to be made if you should happen to come across the 'perfect' diet. I have one that is fairly close to being the 'perfect' diet. It's really so simple I'm surprised no one has thought of it before. There is a snag to it, it's only for married men. Never eat while the wife's talking; you'll lose pounds that way. And if you don't eat while your wife and mother-in-law are talking, well watch out: you could disappear completely.

I think that the best and safest way to diet from a health point of view, is to count the calories. But if you are considering going on a strict diet it is advisable to seek advice from your doctor first. Go and see mine if you like. He'll tell you to lose six pounds and to give up smoking, then he'll light his pipe, blow smoke in your face, and ask you to help him out of the chair as he seems to be stuck.

Well folks, that's it. If you're going on holiday shortly, now is the time to lose those few pounds. Always remember, 'travel broadens one'. If that is so then Orson Welles must have been all over the world.

A slap around the face for Ernie during one of their BBC shows.

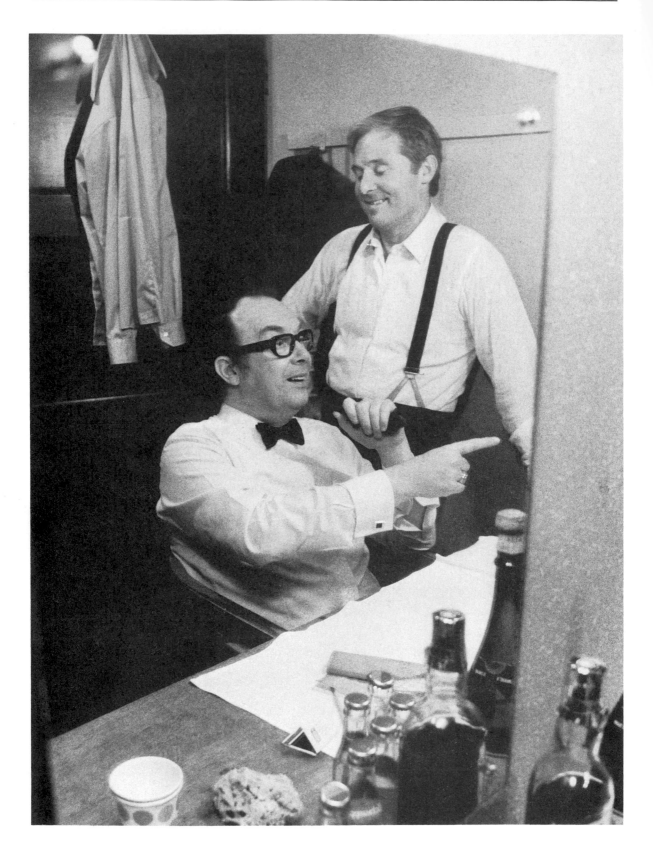

LEFT:
Another town, another show, another dressing room — but still the smiles of performers enjoying themselves.

ABOVE:
A surprise in store at a local scout unveiling ceremony.

ABOVE:
Did people really wear shirts like that in the seventies?

RIGHT:
Eric as a clown on a BBC show.

LEFT:
At a local event in the seventies. I am not sure who the hand belongs to.

ABOVE:
'Not now, Arthur.' Arthur Tolcher, all those years later.

ABOVE:

A BBC Christmas show with guest star Diana Rigg. This was filmed near Banbury, Oxfordshire, very close to where my brother, Steven, was at school.

RIGHT:

Dressed different ways for tennis.

A typical scene from the sketches of the seventies.

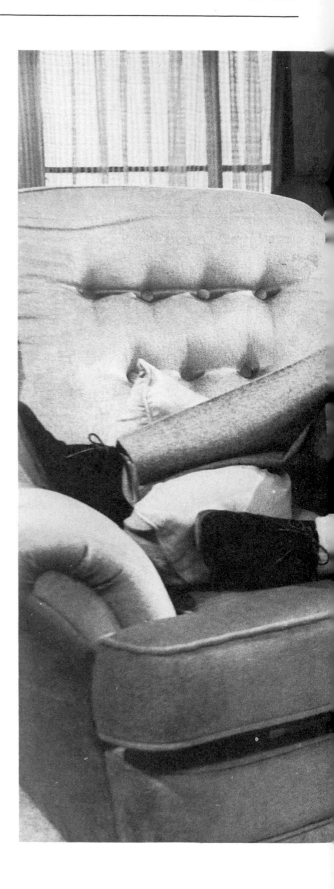

ABOVE:
Guest star Robert Morley, who, when working with Morecambe and Wise, arranged for a lunch hamper to be delivered to the studios from Fortnum and Mason. There was much mutual respect between the duo and the actor, although I think he was the only guest who refused to do a dance routine when offered the chance.

RIGHT:
A legendary sketch with a legendary star. Glenda Jackson was one of the most famous guest stars ever.

OVERLEAF — LEFT:
With Ann Hamilton and Francis Matthews in a BBC show. Ann appeared in numerous Morecambe and Wise shows whenever a female character part was needed. Francis worked with them several times, including on the sixties film The Intelligence Men.

RIGHT:

A Thames Christmas show with guest star Rula Lenska in a sketch called 'The Yukon', *in which Eric and Ernie played gold prospectors.*

An aviation sketch from a Christmas show.

With guest star Eric Porter, who thought he wouldn't be able to dance, and then turned out to be excellent.

Eric and Ernie as members of the Salvation Army, with guest star David Dimbleby.

OVERLEAF — LEFT:
A still from a dance routine during a Thames show. George Chisholm was the guest star.

OVERLEAF — RIGHT:
The move from the BBC to Thames Television seemed to cause a national crisis, judging by the front page of the Evening Standard *in January 1978.*

WEEKEND STANDARD

Evening Standard

LATE PRICES STOP PRESS

47,563   London: Friday January 27 1978   6   8p

COMMUTER STANDARD

London bus fares to go up 1p

By Michael King

RED ARROW fares up 2p to 12p. Most other bus trips up 1p to a minimum 8p.

Fewer miles for your money on the Tube—but a better deal for travellers in the suburbs.

These are the main ingredients of the next round of bus and Underground fare rises due on June 18.

London Transport, obeying GLC instructions, has pegged the rises to an average of 10 per cent, matching inflation and keeping within Government guidelines.

They will cost Londoners £13 million later this year and £25 million more a year thereafter.

The package still has to be approved by the Price Commission and the Greater London Council.

Changeover

London Transport wants to increase the maximum off-peak Tube fare for pensioners from 20p to 25p and the children's bus flat fare from 5p to 6p. Mr Mote will call for their rejection when the fares are debated by his committee next Thursday.

The rest of the package is likely to be approved by County Hall Tories.

Coin machines on Red Arrow buses are designed to take more than one coin—they already work on two 5p pieces. Only a small adjustment is needed for them to take a 2p piece along with 10p. The cost of the changeover is minimal, says London Transport.

● Commuter forum Page 2, Commuter Standard Page 8

MORECAMBE AND WISE SWITCH TO ITV

By Peter Atkinson

MORECAMBE and Wise–the BBC's biggest stars with a Christmas audience of 28 million – have signed an exclusive two-year contract with ITV.

BBC Light Entertainment head James Gilbert—"We wish them well."

They have agreed to do four shows a year and a major film for Thames.

Their defection is a massive blow to the BBC, even more so because the comedy duo will now be doing a 1978 Christmas show on Thames TV.

BBC light entertainment executives learnt yesterday that their fight to keep Morecambe and Wise had failed. It is understood it was not money which lured them away, but the prospect of the film.

The BBC would probably have matched any cash offer Thames could make but not the film. Thames has its own film company, Euston Films, which made The Sweeney.

The BBC's head of light entertainment, Mr James Gilbert said today: "The BBC is not a film company and cannot compete with an offer which links a feature film to a TV contract.

"Obviously we are sorry to lose Eric and Ernie, after so many years but we wish them well."

Mr Gilbert will now have to find a new star to fill the schedule. He has one consolation, Mike Yarwood. Last Christmas, according to ITV he did better than Morecambe and Wise, a fact disputed by the BBC at the time.

The film attraction for the comedians is that

ERIC AND ERNIE . . . signed to Thames for four shows and a major feature film.

it will help them build a reputation in the United States. Eric and Ernie have always been disappointed that the BBC has not been able to sell their shows in the lucrative U.S. market.

The new Morecambe and Wise shows will be the responsibility of Mr Philip Jones, head of light entertainment at Thames.

He plans to make the show as different as possible from the BBCs format.

Thames's managing director, Mr Bryan Cow-

Cont. Back Page Col. 1

Lester: Police search home

By Ian Glover-James

DETECTIVES started a close search today of the Reading home of runaway Lester Chapman, eight, who has been missing for 15 days.

A team of police called on Lester's mother, 25-year-old Mrs Linda Chapman, — just 1.0 p.m. reinforced by scene-of-crime officers in a police estate-car.

The van loaded two cases of forensic equipment. Photographic and lighting equipment remained in the vehicle.

A CID officer said: "We are making a thorough search of the house and garden." He refused to elaborate.

The Chapmans' modern council house stands at the end of a terrace on the Coley Park Estate—two miles south-west of the city centre.

Police were understood to be interestd in a close examina-

tion of the interior and the 28ft. by 12ft. back garden—which is half-concrete, half lawn—with a small, bare vegetable patch.

It was revealed today that Lester's stepfather was interviewed for a second time by detectives at Reading police station last night.

Letters : 2 ● Londoner's Diary : 16 ● TV and radio : 18, 19 ● Entertainment : 26 ● City : 42 ● Sport : 44

129

ABOVE:
In 1970 Eric was voted Pipeman of the Year, an award he shared with fellow pipe-smoker Manny Shinwell. Here Ernie assists him.

RIGHT:
With guest star Cliff Richard caught in a dance routine for a BBC show. During rehearsal Eric had his head gashed by a prop mop which was thrown to him off-screen. Unfortunately it was thrown like a spear and not in the vertical position as planned.

OVERLEAF:
Eric and Ernie, back together again after Eric comes back from Harefield hospital where he'd had open-heart surgery. The furry thing crawling across his top lip came as a shock to all of us. The small picture shows the card he had at the end of his bed while in hospital: he used the pseudonym of George Wilson to avoid attracting attention. M.H. Yacoub is the famous Egyptian surgeon who carried out his op.

George Wilson.

Mr. M. H. YACOUB

ABOVE:

Eric with the Karlin triplets, plus Mrs Waters (mother of London Management publicist Eddie), and Mike Fountain, Eric's driver, en route to do a 'bank raid' in Yarmouth. Eric arranged a champagne picnic to put a bit of sparkle into the day. The Karlins worked several of the Morecambe and Wise tour shows during the seventies as well as appearing on one of their TV programmes.

During the tour shows, if visiting a coastal town Eric would more often than not buy a load of crab claws which he'd eat in his car on the way home. Mike told me it must have made a bizarre sight seeing a Rolls Royce cruising up the motorway, crab claws flying out the window.

On one occasion they were waved down by the police. They thought it was for speeding, but it turned out the police had recognized the car and Eric and wanted his autograph.

ABOVE:
Awards are always appreciated as icing on the cake when you've enjoyed and endured a long, illustrious career. The metal one at the back, which is supposed to resemble a smiling face, was for Personality of the Year, which Eric and Ernie received several times over the years. Pictured with the two awards (the other is from the Variety Club) are invitations to various shows.

CHARITIES AND COMFORTS

October 29

The other day I bought a book on British birds and found it most interesting. I sit by the lounge window with the field-glasses and bird watch — I've made a list at the back of the birds I've seen so far in my garden.

Fishing was a very relaxing and enjoyable pastime for my father — except when he was unsuccessful, as on the following occasions!

My younger brother, Steven, is a keen fisherman. Because he showed an interest in the sport, where I had not. I think my father felt obliged to nurture it. He took him fishing on the Test. They'd been angling downstream for two hours without a bite. 'I argued with dad that we should try upstream,' recalled Steven, who then was only a young boy. 'We argued for about ten minutes, then he finally gave in. Nothing happened upstream either, so we ended up blaming the river.'

There was another time when Steven had gone fishing with him. 'Dad had had to go off for a few minutes,' he said. 'When he returned it was to see me wrestling with the biggest fish I'd ever had on the line. I began shaking with excitement and panic: this was a surprise catch and if I landed it, a very special one. Because I began panicking dad clipped me round the ear and told me not to be so stupid, that I was going to lose it. This made me all the more careless. Eventually it broke the line and escaped, much to dad's displeasure. In fact he told me I'd been exaggerating how big it was — but I hadn't been.'

David Fynsong went on a fishing trip with Eric to Little Tringford Reservoir in Hertfordshire, and it made a great impression on him. Here is an extract from the account he wrote of the day they spent together.

The fishery is arranged so that to fish the water you have to walk along a small jetty and then step onto a floating platform. At eleven-thirty I heard a familiar voice.
'Is this little Tring?' the voice said to a nearby angler. I looked around to see that Eric's interruption had made this chap cast badly and his fly line was draped around his ears and hat.

We started to chat and decided to fish on the bank we were on. I asked Eric if he found much time for fishing. 'Well, I do as much fishing as I can, but I rarely go for a drink afterwards, although I own shares in various pubs and hotels. You'd lose me in a crowd, but the moment I open my mouth and say something, it's a dead giveaway; it's the voice. If I go into a pub with everyone talking, it falls silent, just like flicking a switch. They all stop and look. That's one reason I don't fish public waters. Much as I like talking to people, I need my spare time to fish. I usually end up talking for an hour with six blokes I've never met in my life when I could be catching fish!' He looked at me and laughed. I saw his fly containers and, to my surprise, here was a collection of Tic Tac boxes, an old tin from Woolies from the year dot and a clear plastic box of the sort that you would buy throat lozenges in from a chemist. I found out from Joan later that Eric felt very guilty about spending money on fishing. During our subsequent conversations it became clear that Eric was concerned about getting value for money in everything he bought, but especially fishing tackle and fishing clothing. He explained, 'When I was a boy, my father had to scrimp and save for our family, and those days have never left me. Even on the odd occasion when I gamble and win, I stop, spend my profit on something like this (he fingered his fly-fishing waistcoat) and then go back and gamble my original stake. That way I have something to show for my efforts.'

We picked a good spot on the first platform and began fishing. Eric was sitting on a lightweight collapsible stool. When he retrieved his line, bent slightly forward with his pipe protruding from his mouth, he looked like one of the reservoir herons, bent on destruction.

Eventually, as we were having no luck we came ashore and retired to the boat park, an area of shingle just past the second stage. One of the other syndicate members arrived on the scene along with Bernard the bailiff and his son Graham.

'Hello there, it's been a long time', said Eric to Bernard.

'It must be seven years since you were last this way', replied Bernard as they shook hands. Eric looked at Graham.

'How old are you?' he asked.

'Fifteen', replied Graham.

'Are you married?' came back Eric sharply. Poor Graham was dumbstruck, and the rest of us laughed. By this time Eric had unfolded his chair and sat down by this small gathering. Reaching for a cheese sandwich, he held it to his lips like a mouth organ and said to Graham, 'I'll play you a tune.'

The little group melted away, which left the two of us alone again. We had by now both demolished our respective snacks and drinks, so we gathered our rods, bags, panniers, nets and so on, and made a move along the shingle path, talking about writing and books.

'So how do you write a book?', I enquired.

'Well, I use a typewriter. I tend to type with one finger, but in capitals. I tried putting the text down on a cassette recorder, but it takes ages once you put in all the full stops and commas. I've even tried dictation but that takes just as long, so I type it myself. My book *Mr Lonely* got into the bestseller list. Another thing I found out recently was that our 1977 Christmas show was in the *Guinness Book of Records* for the largest audience at any one time in the UK: twenty-eight million.' He raised his eyebrows slightly, grinned and looked a bit like a very contented cat. By now we had arrived at the first platform on the north bank. We dropped our gear, and began to do battle with the unseen adversary. Eric had shown me a fly of American origin that would have made Izaac Walton turn in his grave and banned for life on some waters ... but not here!

'You know, it's important to keep in the public eye. Ernie and I don't do as much television as before so you have to make enough appearances to be recognized. I do *What's My Line*; I go on, be myself, like I am here, and twelve million people see me every week. All I do is turn up.' I felt there was a little more to it than that. 'You see,' he continued, 'If I walk down the street and nobody recognizes me, I'm no longer a star.' Eric then turned sideways on and with his free right hand looked at me, emphasizing every word of the next sentence with his right hand. 'You have to be a star.'

I then asked Eric about other people's writing, and he took the opportunity to relate a little story about opinions.

'Opinions count for nothing, David. A young lad, a son of a neighbour of ours, 'phoned me up one night. "Oh, Mr Morecambe," he said, "I wonder if you could read a script I've written? I'm thinking of sending it to ITV." "But why do you want my opinion?" I asked. He told me he thought that if he said Eric Morecambe had read it, that might help. I said to him, "If I like it, they might not. On the other hand if I don't like it, they might. Don't forget you're talking to the man who told Gracie Fields not to sing 'Sally'." He didn't know what I was talking about.'

Once again we went our separate ways and set about trying to tempt a trout ...

Eric's involvement with and love of Luton Town FC are well known. He wrote about it in the article that follows, and goes on to give an account of a Lord's Taverners function.

I am better known as a comedian than a sportsman — people prove it constantly with expressions like 'that's Eric Morecambe, he's with Luton'. Morecambe and Luton — it has the ring of a cheap-day return.

I have spent many happy minutes with Luton Town FC. I used to be a director of the club, but no longer: after six years (third division to first, to second) I found that work and worry were becoming a little too much, so I gave up my directorship and now I'm a vice president — which means I get one free seat instead of four, and, if we lose, much less aggravation. Whatever happens, I shall always follow 'my team'.

It's amazing how many people in show business want to be in some way connected with sport. Myself, it's Luton, Lord's Taverners, MCC, Goaldiggers — and I've appeared on *Pot Black*, cup finals at Wembley and spent a whole afternoon with Dickie Davis on his *World of Sport*. There have been many dinners and luncheons — all most enjoyable. I've met the people who run the games and the people who are the games; I've had lunch with Ron Greenwood and the whole of the staff and players of the England team, and I didn't have to work — just be there. I was given a whole England soccer outfit except the boots (I take seven on the left leg and nine on the right, so they wouldn't split a pair). A thousand memories, all because I was asked by a man called Tony Hunt, then chairman of Luton, if I would join the board, and when I did most of my friends thought I was mad. In the last ten years I have been in the two most wonderful businesses in the world — show business and sport.

But I'm not the only entertainer keen on sport. Take Elton John (affectionately known as the Watford Gap), he's very sport-orientated — it's the way he walks ... Pete Murray — he's the one who supports Arsenal — well, the first four letters are right. How many people know that Marty Feldman is a tennis fanatic? He can actually go to Wimbledon and watch a game without moving his head.

Ernie Wise, who once thought Billy Bremner was the Chancellor of West Germany, now Ernie follows Clydebank, Barclays Bank and Nat. West Ham.

How many times have we watched the pro-am golf on the TV? Wonderful matches, with people like Gary Player and Lee Trevino playing little Olga Corbett of the Two Ronnies, and Sean Coronary.

It's like the old saying that actors want to be comics and comics want to be actors: well, it's the same with sport. Show people want to be sportsmen and sportsmen want to be show people — Freddie Trueman is well known for his after-dinner speaking — when he speaks, he's usually after dinner. It's also a well-known fact that Rachel Heyhoe Flint knows more dirty jokes than Freddie — and that's saying something.

That brings me on to another thing: we seem to forget that sport is not all men. Women play cricket, football, tennis — almost every game, and in my opinion they bring glamour into any sport. And look at the small amount of clothes they wear: my grandmother went to bed in more clothes than Virginia Wade won Wimbledon in.

One of the best things that happened to me in sport is being the president of the Lord's Taverners. It is a charity organization that was started through cricket, although now it has added golf and boxing to its Patrick Mower bosom. The Lord's Taverners has a list of names of both sport and show-business personalities longer than Nelson's right arm. Mr Tim Brooke-Taylor — there's three for a start; Willie Rushton, with his flaming red beard — the last time I saw anything like that on a face the whole herd had to be destroyed.

Tim Rice, co-author of such great hits as 'Patrick Moore Super Star' and 'Ryvita' — in fact, anyone in showbiz who is anyone is in the Taverners. And don't forget that behind every star is a surprised wife. These stars give up their spare and precious time to work for us so that we may give to under-privileged children. We give playing fields, coaches for the handicapped, cricket facilities for the youth — all this takes a lot of money and a lot of money takes a lot of finding.

As I've already said, not everyone in the Taverners is in show business. There are many famous sportsmen and women who belong. I mean, how's this for name dropping: the Nawab of Pataudi — eh? Be honest — how about that? I remember once having a drink with his sirocco; I was on neat gin and crisps, and he was on Indian tonic and popadams as always. The conversation got round to cricket and I asked him a direct question about a certain English player. Now for at least half a minute he couldn't answer, he just looked at me with his face going slowly red and his eyes bulging — evidently a piece of popadam had slipped down the wrong way. I slapped his back and the offending object flew across the room and landed in the mina bird's cage. This mina bird ate it and never spoke again. I repeated the question. 'What do you think of Bedser?' and the Nawab said 'I don't sleep on bed, sir, I sleep on rush mat'. The Nawab lives in New Delhi, near India and next to Nicholas Parsons.

Of course, the Taverners have certain rules. I can remember two: one is that Des O'Connor can never be a member, and the second is that we do not allow political jokes, because sometimes they get elected.

All our members eagerly await April, knowing that soon we will thrill to the sound of leather hitting Brian Close. Prince Charles was our last President, while at the moment I'm your last (that doesn't sound quite right) ... President.

Prince Philip (by the way he can verify the Nawab story — next time you see him just ask) is our twelfth man — that means if we are ever short we ring up the Palace and ask the Queen if he can come out and play. She's very good about letting him come with us on Sundays, except if he has to mow the lawn before one of their garden parties.

Freddie Trueman plays for us as often as he can. Fred is known as a quickie — but nowadays that's usually after the game.

Every Sunday in the cricket season we play a team for charity, and the kindness and hospitality shown to us by our hosts is tremendous. Everyone enjoys themself so much ... usually an enormous marquee is put up for our players and their friends and their players and their friends. In this marquee we have lunch, tea and drinks — but not necessarily in that order. There are always lots of stars to be seen, both male and female — and let me tell you this, sunshine: if you are invited into that marquee, your year is made. You will see, do and hear things your vicar wouldn't believe.

You could bump into Geoff Boycott, to some people, a genius, to others, not a genius. To me it depends on how you define the word genius. A genius can be a nudist with a memory for faces — or Geoff Boycott. You could bump into Barry Sheene, John Conteh, Reg Simpson, Bill Edrich, John Snow, Dennis Compton, and if you're lucky you could bump into Pauline Collins (she plays Thomas in *George and Mildred*). You might bump into Patrick Moore. Now he has a devastating googly which in all probability has been caused by his run-up — or the fact that he's put his cricket box in upside down. You might bump into Ronnie Barker or trip over Ronnie Corbett ... eat a waiter with Donald Pleasance ... have a drink with Colin Milburn ... write a song with Michael Margolis FRSA, MSTD, MADCL, MISA ... pick a fight with Noël Gordon ... all this can be done before you sit down to lunch or the game starts. And the food is home-cooking, which is where a lot of the men in the marquee think their wives are.

Imagine it's July, a boiling hot afternoon, ruined only by the pouring rain and the wind. You have been honoured: you are wearing a Taverners' name tab — this has your name on it. Also you will wear a name tab on one of your socks — that's so that if you end up under the table, you'll know who you are. If through having a few too many you lose the name tab on your jacket, make sure you take your sock with the other name tab on it off, otherwise only half of you is sent back home. But at the moment you are sober and you keep your eye on the tent flap as star after star weaves in through the crowd.

You are standing by the bar at one end of the marquee. It's early yet — 11.45 a.m. to be exact. You've been standing in line for the last fifteen minutes waiting your turn to get a drink. 'A gin-and-tonic, please', you beam. 'With ice?' You grin 'no ice'. The lady who serves you grimaces. The thing to do then is not to say anything but just let her look at your glass and you'll feel it go cold in your hand, and if you're going to stay on gin-and-tonic and you happen to be one of the lucky early ones who gets a piece of lemon — hold on to it, and the same applies to the glass. Keep it with you at all times, even though you hold it up to the sun and you can't see the drink in it for your finger prints. But watch out for your lemon: there have been more lemon slices stolen on these occasions than money.

You walk away from this bar through the long grass underfoot. You are in the holy of holies. You have a drink, two name tabs, a piece of lemon and a smell of the country coming from your shoes. You are now at liberty to talk or listen to anyone. The lemon in your drink is as good as being a mason. Suddenly the marquee flap opens and a man enters with an old cricket bag; you are taken back almost fifty years: a hero of your youth — and he was getting on a bit then. I'm not going to say how old this ex-England player is, it wouldn't be fair; suffice it to say he was there when the great W.G. Grace said 'Son — I think I'll

grow a beard' and what he lacks in muscle he makes up for in flab. He heads straight for the bar.

You walk around the marquee and you hear snatches of conversation.

Major Well I'll tell you this, old fruit: I never had any, er — you know — er, relationships with my wife before we were married. How about you, eh?

Major Star I don't know, what was your wife's maiden name?

The place is beginning to fill, and lunch is in 40 minutes: just about time to get another drink. At this bar will be a group of people whom you have never seen on film, TV or colour radio — unknown to you, these men will probably be the Lord's Taverners council — they may be having a debate. Now debate to them is something you catch de fish with.

After lunch the game starts. You, through having two name tabs and a piece of lemon, can go and stand in the enclosure, a roped off yard to stop people from touching or getting too near the stars. It will be packed because the ropes are on the ground as the man whose job it is to keep them up and stop the people from touching the stars is also their umpire. You may be fortunate enough to stand next to an ex-England cricket star and watch him being sick — let me add that this is not caused by drink. This is what at some time or another we all suffer from — nerves. But now in front of maybe fifty or sixty people, this cricketer has to face Arthur Askey, who is five for seventy-seven — that's his height and age. I would advise you to go back into the marquee and watch a fight between an actor who got the part and one who thought *he* should have got it. Suddenly you hear rapturous applause as Askey has claimed the sick ex-England star cricketer — who is now walking back to the pavilion. The next man is due in — no, we've declared at 151 for 13. It's tea.

You rush towards the tea urn; the woman serving you looks directly at you — it's the same woman who served you the gin-and-tonic. She hands you your tea — it's as cold as your mother-in-law's kiss.

One of our stars has been hurt. A cake has fallen on his foot — an ambulanceman comes over to attend to it: he must be ninety-four or ninety-five — he couldn't put a dressing on a salad.

You hear scattered conversation.
Star Waitress — what's on this plate in case I have to describe it to the doctor?
And then,
Woman If he had really loved me he'd have married someone else.

Today you have been part of the Lord's Taverners — you have mixed with stars, you have talked to beautiful women, you have contributed. It does not matter who wins the game as long as we do. It's getting dusk, it's going-home time. A star gets into his chauffeur-driven Rolls with a beautiful lady. The car won't start, the chauffeur lifts the bonnet, the star and the beautiful lady go back to the marquee. The Taverners motto is being taken down 'Sleep is best, next to a beautiful woman'.

One more drink and back to the Rolls. The chauffeur is still tinkering with the car ... the beautiful woman speaks — 'Would you like a screwdriver?' The chauffeur replies, 'You're very kind madam, but I'd like to get the car started first'.

Prince of entertainers, Eric Morecambe, OBE., President Lords Taverners accompanies Princess Michael of Kent at the Lord's Taverners Annual Ball. Close behind, Joan Morecambe and Prince Michael.

LEFT:
The Lord's Taverners charity was very important to my father, and, I believe, he still holds the record for running three consecutive seasons as their President. There is an association between the Taverners and the Royal Family: HRH The Prince of Wales honoured them by being the first President, and HRH The Prince Philip holds the honorary title of twelfth man.

Besides the Lord's Taverners' newsletters in this photograph, there are Eric's Director's passes for Luton Town FC. He was a very keen supporter.

ABOVE:
A session signing cricket bats for the Lord's Taverners with Edward Heath.

OVERLEAF — LEFT:
Eric looking tremendously convincing as he pretends to play the clarinet.

OVERLEAF — RIGHT:
Trying to synchronize his watch — but shouldn't the earphones be under the hat rather than over?

At a charity football match with Prince Philip.

Prince Charles joins Eric and Ernie on stage
during a Royal performance.

ABOVE:
*At home surrounded by his fishing
equipment, apparently giving my dog,
Bowler, a strict warning about something.*

RIGHT:
*Eric enjoying himself in baseball kit in
Florida in 1981. Note the Mickey Mouse
watch.*

Eric continued his link with Harefield hospital, where his open-heart surgery was performed. This photograph was taken at a sponsored jog — in which he ran all of five yards.

Pretending to be playing football for Luton Town FC. In fact he is kicking a ball around with some lads at a local school.

THE CHANCELLOR
WILL DECLARE THE CONGREGATION OPEN

A Trumpet Fanfare will be played

———————

CONFERMENT OF INITIAL DEGREES

The Chancellor will then confer the degree of Bachelor of Arts on members of
Lonsdale College, who will be presented by the Principal, Professor E. H. Lloyd.

The Chancellor will then confer the degree of Bachelor of Science on members of
Lonsdale College, who will be presented by the Principal, Professor E. H. Lloyd.

The Chancellor will then confer the degree of Bachelor of Education on members
of S. Martin's College of Education, who will be presented by the Principal,
Mr. R. Clayton.

(The Congregation is asked to reserve applause until all the members of a college
have been admitted to a specified degree)

CONFERMENT OF HONORARY DEGREES

The Chancellor will then confer the following Honorary Degrees:

DOCTOR OF LETTERS *(Honoris Causa)*
Mr. J. Eric Bartholomew

DOCTOR OF LAWS *(Honoris Causa)*
Professor Harry Lawson

DOCTOR OF LETTERS *(Honoris Causa)*
Dr. Aylmer Macartney

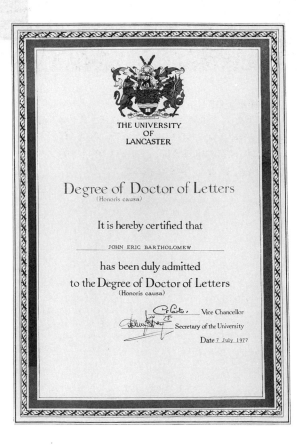

THE UNIVERSITY
OF
LANCASTER

Degree of Doctor of Letters
(Honoris causa)

It is hereby certified that

JOHN ERIC BARTHOLOMEW

has been duly admitted
to the Degree of Doctor of Letters
(Honoris causa)

Vice Chancellor
Secretary of the University
Date 7 July 1977

LEFT — ABOVE AND BELOW:
In July 1977 Eric was awarded an honorary degree by the University of Lancaster. It was something that meant more to him than almost any other achievement.

ABOVE:
At Lancaster just after receiving the degree from Princess Alexandra.

ABOVE:

Artist Richard Stone is pictured here with Eric and the portrait he painted for a documentary programme. Eric kept the painting after the programme went out.

RIGHT:

More fun with a favourite hobby.

These two photographs were taken during the final moments of Eric's life. He was performing at the Rose Theatre in Tewkesbury, Gloucestershire, with Stan Stennett (shown here), who worked with Morecambe and Wise as far back as the early fifties (see page 50). Eric collapsed and died shortly after coming off stage.

PICTURE CREDITS

Every effort has been made to trace primary sources of photographs. In the few cases where this has not been possible, Queen Anne Press wish to apologize if the acknowledgement proves to be inadequate; in no case is this intentional. If any owner of copyright who has remained untraced will communicate with Queen Anne Press a reasonable fee will be paid and the required acknowledgement made in any future editions of the book.

Unless otherwise specified, all other photographs by members and friends of the Morecambe family. Michael Barrington-Martin: 48-9; *Bedford County Press*: 111; BBC Enterprises Ltd: 59, 104, 109, 110, 112, 113, 115, 116, 117, 120, 122, 124-5, 126, 127, 131; *Daily Express*: 147, 148; *Echo & Post*, Hemel Hempstead: 92B; Jack Emerald: 40; *Evening Standard*: 129; Frank: 39; Jon Graeme Photography: 114; *Hertfordshire Advertiser*: 98; Jack Hylton: 28; Jeff Jones: 145; *Lancashire Evening Post*: 155; Robin Laurance: 130; Doug McKenzie: 85A, 149; Mirrorpic: 90-1; Photo Source: 79; Press Association: 121; Rimis: 36-7; Robin: 58; South Bedfordshire News Agency: 70; *Sun* Newspaper: 132-3, 157 (Photo Hobden); Thames T.V.: 88, 123, 128, 146; A. Todd: 35; The *Visitor*, Morecambe: 103; A.C.K. Ware: 65; Eddie Waters: 82, 134